STUDENT ENGAGEMENT AND THE ACADEMIC LIBRARY

STUDENT ENGAGEMENT AND THE ACADEMIC LIBRARY

Loanne Snavely, Editor

LIBRARIES UNLIMITED

AN IMPRINT OF ABC-CLIO, LLC
Santa Barbara, California • Denver, Colorado • Oxford, England

Copyright 2012 by ABC-CLIO, LLC

All rights reserved. No part of this publication may be reproduced, stored in a retrieval system, or transmitted, in any form or by any means, electronic, mechanical, photocopying, recording, or otherwise, except for the inclusion of brief quotations in a review, or reproducibles, which may be copied for classroom and educational programs only, without prior permission in writing from the publisher.

Library of Congress Cataloging-in-Publication Data

Student engagement and the academic library / Loanne Snavely, editor.
pages cm
Includes bibliographical references and index.
ISBN 978–1–59884–983–7 (pbk.) — ISBN 978–1–59884–984–4 (ebook) (print) 1. Academic libraries—United States. 2. Libraries and colleges—United States. 3. Libraries and students—United States. 4. Academic libraries—United States—Marketing. 5. Academic libraries—Public relations—United States. 6. Library orientation for college students—United States. 7. Information literacy—Study and teaching (Higher)—United States. 8. Research—Methodology—Study and teaching (Higher)—United States. I. Snavely, Loanne.
Z675.U5S8334 2012
027.70973—dc23   2012014939

ISBN: 978–1–59884–983–7
EISBN: 978–1–59884–984–4

16 15 14 13 12   1 2 3 4 5

This book is also available on the World Wide Web as an eBook.
Visit www.abc-clio.com for details.

Libraries Unlimited
An Imprint of ABC-CLIO, LLC

ABC-CLIO, LLC
130 Cremona Drive, P.O. Box 1911
Santa Barbara, California 93116-1911

This book is printed on acid-free paper ∞

Manufactured in the United States of America

Contents

Acknowledgments		vii
Introduction		ix
1.	Engaging Undergraduates with the Academic Library *Loanne Snavely, Head, Library Learning Services, Penn State University Libraries*	1
2.	Using an Alternate Reality Game to Engage Students in Learning *Emily Rimland, Information Literacy Librarian, Penn State University Libraries*	11
3.	*Lost in the Stacks:* The Research Library Rock 'n' Roll Radio Show! *Ameet Doshi, Head, User Experience Librarian and Assessment Coordinator, Georgia Institute of Technology Library*	23
4.	Perceived Ease of Use and Student Satisfaction and Engagement with the Library *Lesley Moyo, Director for Research & Instructional Services, University Libraries, Virginia Tech*	31
5.	Invisible Connections: Creating Community through Oral Storytelling in the UAS Listening Project *Wendy Girven, Public Services Librarian/Assistant Professor of Library Science, University of Alaska Southeast*	41

6.	Engaging Undergraduates in Research: Exploring Students' Research Behavior and Rewarding Outstanding Use of Library Resources	51
	Emily Daly, Coordinator of Upper Level Instruction and Librarian for the Program in Education, Duke University	
7.	Undergraduates of Opportunity: Capitalizing on Talent and Crafting Undergraduate Projects with Rare Books and Manuscripts	63
	Sandra Stelts, Curator of Rare Books and Manuscripts, Penn State University Libraries	
8.	Engaging International Students with the Academic Library	71
	Dawn Amsberry, Reference and Instruction Librarian, Penn State University Libraries	
9.	Service Learning: Engaging College Students with the Library and Information Literacy Competencies	85
	Maureen Barry, Librarian for First-Year and Distance Learning Services, Wright State University	
10.	Developing a Marketing Plan for the Library by and for Students	95
	Gary W. White, Head of Reference Collections and Research, Penn State University Libraries	
11.	MInDSpace: New Media, Mashups, and Learning	105
	Jacqueline M. Fritz, Instructor, Learning Technologies Liaison, Bucks County Community College	
12.	The Library as Studio: Enculturation, Student Engagement, and the Spaces of the Library	119
	Patrick Tomlin, Art and Architecture Librarian, Virginia Tech	
Index		131
About the Editor and Contributors		137

Acknowledgments

I would like to thank the many librarians with whom I visited as I traveled to academic libraries to explore their innovative programs and spaces. Thanks to the authors who were willing to share their exciting student-centered initiatives for this book and to Dawn Amsberry for her assistance in formatting references for the chapters. And, finally, thanks to my family for their patience during my many hours at the computer.

Introduction

Academic libraries are facing a rapidly evolving landscape in every facet of their responsibilities and influence. Technology and the capabilities ensuing from new developments are changing the way information is produced, used and perceived by students. While the core mission and offerings of academic libraries may remain in the high-quality services and resources they provide, the challenge of engaging students in their use increases annually and, it seems, exponentially. To succeed in the emerging landscape that is our contemporary society, ways must be found to remain relevant and vibrant in students' academic careers.

Finding these paths requires librarians to be creative in ways they have never dreamed and to innovate with enthusiasm. Libraries are steeped in tradition, and while librarians were often at the forefront of early automation efforts, they have often been less responsive to the need for engaging students as the rate of change increases and the need to respond quickly becomes urgent. Innovation and creativity must be championed and the spirit of change embraced if libraries are to remain at the heart of the educational enterprise.

Craig Gibson began the conversation in 2006 in his book *Student Engagement and Information Literacy*. Gibson's conversation on engaging students with information literacy will be continued and broadened throughout this book to examine activities, projects, initiatives, and spaces that create student engagement with academic libraries across a wide spectrum. Some examples come from Penn State, while others come from libraries whose librarians are creating exciting and innovative programs and initiatives. In each case, they have been chosen as examples of innovative ways of engaging undergraduate students with academic libraries.

As Google takes center stage in perceived information provision worldwide and students become accustomed to lightning-quick and super easy information searching, librarians must take seriously their need to win students over to their offerings and engage them with their resources and services. This will become an increasingly challenging task, and one that deserves focused attention now.

This book will document the successes of those in the forefront of this wave, authors new to the profession or with many years' experience, and those whose programs and initiatives engage students with libraries, with the idea of a library, with information literacy, with the research process, and with library spaces, services, programs and concepts as well as the marketing efforts that are drawing them in. These authors tell their stories by weaving in the students' own voices to record the engagement and relevance of these initiatives. The affective outcomes and positive attitudes that these efforts spawn are key to the future of student success with more in-depth research resources in their disciplines, which in turn ensures the continued central place of libraries as the heart of the academy.

A SPECIAL WORLD THE AUDIENCE CAN TRULY ENJOY

While librarians do not think of libraries as competing with the world of entertainment, Dr. Peggy Van Pelt, a Disney Imagineer, reminded us that libraries do compete with myriad other possibilities for students' time—from their academic work to the world of entertainment, relationships, gaming, and fun. She states: "I know from the work we do at Walt Disney Imagineering that it takes a highly talented, focused group of committed people to transform the world of ideas into a successful environment or a special world that the audience can truly enjoy" (2000, 93). Her prophetic statements at that time are even more relevant today than they were when she shared them at an Association of College and Research Libraries (ACRL) program. Librarians must ensure that they remain relevant, appealing, and welcoming in physical and virtual presences, keeping current with trends and exploring how those trends might mesh with the goals of the library. Libraries must be handy (in their spaces) and easy to use. Once engaged initially, feeling positive about the library and its resources, and having had success in finding and using information purposefully, students are much more willing to dig deeply and fully engage with academic information resources as they advance in their majors.

In Chapter 1, the information literacy continuum is presented and the importance of placing significant attention on the first level is shown. This points to nurturing a positive, affective attitude toward the library, and sets the stage for the real learning ahead. The creativity and innovation required of librarians to achieve this is an area not frequently championed in libraries in the past but will become increasingly critical as librarians seek to hold and advance their position at the heart of an institution of higher education. A variety of ideas and approaches are presented that can positively influence these early affective attitudes and prepare students for the information literacy strategies they will soon be learning and sets the stage for the following chapters.

ALTERNATE REALITY

One area that has been showing great potential in integrating fun into the educational enterprise is games and gaming. One conference speaker several years ago advised librarians not to mess up the fun of tournaments and games by trying to insert library content. While there may be some value in the pure fun of hosting commercial games, I believe there is a much greater value in the opportunity to engage students with libraries through the content of the games.

In Chapter 2, Emily Rimland writes about a homegrown game on a scale accessible to academic libraries—an Alternate Reality Game (ARG) created collaboratively by library faculty and staff and with input from gamers and others on campus that focused on integrating library learning goals. She explores ideas to acquaint students with elements of library research and information literacy in a fun way. Rather than just a game for game's sake, this approach emphasizes students' critical thinking skills and librarians' creativity. Finding an intriguing "rabbit hole," engaging campus partners, developing appropriately challenging quests, tracking progress, and allowing for questions along the way all presented challenges to be solved. The opening scenario begins with a video created collaboratively with campus partners featuring the university president—an innovative way to engage students with the university and the educational enterprise.

RADIO PROGRAMS

Ameet Doshi has integrated fun and entertainment to engage students with the library at Georgia Tech. Ameet partners with the campus student radio station, his library's subject specialists, and campus researchers to bring *Lost in the Stacks* live on air. Each show revolves around a topic, hosts special guests, and features popular music that relates to the topic—all mashed up into a fun and informative radio show. Ameet also discusses an accessible aquarium project, virtual posters on undergraduate research, and some new uses of emerging technologies in Chapter 3.

FINDING MEASURES TO GATHER DATA

Measuring student engagement will be a challenge in the future. Identifying its various aspects and finding measures that can be put in place to gather data will be an ongoing effort. In Chapter 4, Lesley Moyo has made a first step on this path with her research showing that perceived ease of use has a statistically significant correlation with user satisfaction. This research demonstrates that continuing to enhance and streamline services, upgrading user spaces, and concentrating on various factors that enhance the users' experience are worthy endeavors. Much has been written recently about physical library spaces, the information or knowledge commons, media and technology spaces, and other attractive spaces that provide for individual study and group work, plenty of technology, and related services. In addition to physical spaces, efforts to make our webpages, information resources, user guides, and other online resources easy to find and use will help libraries to continue to engage users and bring them into our spaces.

HIGH-IMPACT PRACTICES THAT ENGAGE STUDENTS

George Kuh has studied and published on student engagement in higher education for many years, and he and his colleagues have found that educationally purposeful cocurricular activities are among the most meaningful of a students' undergraduate education (Gonyea and Kuh 2009). This research indicates those activities may provide even more context and meaning than we have previously considered. In particular, he has identified "high impact" activities. Some of these have received significant attention by libraries and in the library literature, including first-year seminars, learning communities, writing-intensive courses, and collaborative work.

Several other high-impact activities have not received as much attention, and innovative projects and initiatives that address these high impact practices will be highlighted in this book. These include common intellectual experiences, undergraduate research, diversity/global learning, service learning or community-based learning, internships, and capstone experiences.

COMMON INTELLECTUAL EXPERIENCES

Common intellectual experiences create meaning for students beyond a single class and help create connections among students from various majors and disciplines. On many campuses, these experiences take the form of a one-book program, which is how this initiative began, but which then grew into very unique and exciting projects. In Chapter 5, Wendy Girven discusses her library's leadership of a common intellectual and community building experience in the form of a One Campus, One Book program focused on the book *Listening Is an Act of Love*. This common reading experience formed the basis for a personalized campus-wide initiative to create their StoryCorp-type program known as the Listening Project. This shared community-wide oral storytelling project created "invisible connections" across campus and involved students in creating, recording, and preserving their own stories, which resulted in a new student-based archival collection for the university.

UNDERGRADUATE RESEARCH

A growing trend in higher education has been to encourage undergraduates in the pursuit of original research, and these experiences have been found to be a high-impact practice that engages students. At Penn State, an Undergraduate Research Exhibition each spring displays the research conducted by undergraduate students from all disciplines. To highlight and recognize the information literacy component of the research and to reward excellence in information literacy, a series of Information Literacy Awards were created in 2008 and are awarded annually. Other awards have been developed to champion the information literacy aspects of the research process at UC–Berkeley, the University of Texas at Austin, St. John Fisher College, Duke University, and Northwestern State University. Emily Daly writes in Chapter 6 about her exploration of undergraduate honors students use of library resources and collections and of Duke University Libraries' information literacy award.

INTERNSHIPS AND SPECIAL COLLECTIONS IN THE RESEARCH PROCESS

Internships can be an exciting disciplinary approach to undergraduate student engagement—an innovative approach for libraries to participate in creating high-impact experiences that engage students on their campuses through the application of disciplinary experiences they have already achieved and allowing them to apply these experiences to solve real-world problems and contribute meaningfully to real projects. An endowment has created paid library internships that enable students to gain professional experience in their discipline while earning course credit in the major. In Chapter 7,

Sandra Stelts writes about her experience with these endowed library internships as well as other ways that undergraduates can become involved in the research process through special collections, rare books and manuscripts, exhibits, etc., by using examples of recent projects, such as early photographic processes and illuminated manuscripts. These experiences allow students to explore original source materials and rare book and archival collections in their areas of interest. Through them, students gain an expertise not normally attainable in an undergraduate program.

DIVERSITY/GLOBAL LEARNING

A component of diversity and global learning that is frequently overlooked is our growing population of international students. Across the country and at Penn State, numbers of international students are growing annually. Traditionally, international graduate students have been the larger populations, but this year, for the first time, Penn State's international undergraduate students have outnumbered them. Engaging this special population with libraries, their services, and collections will be increasingly important for academic libraries. In Chapter 8, Dawn Amsberry shares a variety of programming and initiatives to engage these students and introduce them to the American model of academic libraries by using examples from initiatives at Penn State as well as those used elsewhere. She shares results of a survey revealing programming and outreach activities directed primarily to international student populations in the academic library community.

SERVICE LEARNING

Service learning has received lots of attention in the higher education literature and some modest attention in the library literature. However, a true integration of service learning with information literacy has not been forthcoming. In Chapter 9, Maureen Barry, from Wright State University, discusses a course she developed and has cotaught. This innovative credit-bearing information literacy course integrates service learning in a way that provides a real contribution to the service organization and to students' personal growth and involvement as well as to their increased information literacy abilities and confidence.

APPLICATION OF STUDENT DISCIPLINARY EXPERTISE

In addition to undergraduate research and internships, there are other ways students can share the disciplinary expertise they have already gained with libraries, creating meaningful experiences and helping to engage these students with libraries in a wide variety of ways. It is often the students themselves who know best about what works for them. Asking them can guide us in the right direction.

One disciplinary area in which this is particularly true is in marketing. Marketing the library is an essential component of engaging students, and as mentioned earlier, we must get on students' radar and be a part of their educational landscape from the start. In Chapter 10, Gary W. White discusses the creation of a marketing plan for the library by and for students through input from highly experienced corporate managers in a special MBA marketing class, through undergraduate marketing internships, and through student focus groups.

In addition to programs and activities that relate to Kuh and Gonyea's high-impact practices, other practices are predicted that have not yet been identified but are critical to librarians' success in engaging students.

INTEGRATING MEDIA, INSTRUCTIONAL DESIGN, AND LIBRARY RESOURCES

In Chapter 11, Jackie Fritz shares the Bucks County Community College experience in which a variety of elements have been drawn together in their MInDSpace project and integrated into the library and academic enterprise in an exceptional way. The space includes the equipment (still and flip video cameras, microphones, etc.) and technology needed for creating media projects as well as the assistance students need relating to the library and gathering print and media resources, those relating to instructional design of the project, and finally to the technical details of bringing the student project to reality. In addition, the space itself has a visual impact through the unique and beautiful hand-blown glass lamps that adorn each table, creating a glow and aura that totally removes the normal ambiance commonly felt in a lab and instead transports the user into an emotional space that has an exciting quality, inspiring the creative spirit in the minds at work. Bucks County Community College received the 2010 Excellence in Academic Libraries Award, which recognized this outstanding project. The media mashups created there were inspiring student work.

LIBRARY AS STUDIO

In Chapter 12, Patrick Tomlin explores the studio learning environment and its relationship to the specialized uses of the architecture library as an extension of the classroom and the studio. This vibrant library is embedded literally and figuratively into the architecture curriculum so the collections and the images it contains are available seamlessly and at a moment's notice for students and faculty as they discuss innovative architects, designers, and individual manifestations of their ideas. A space designed for and by architects and their students and located at the heart of their academic program creates a space that truly inspires learning and is a recipe for success.

LOOKING TO THE FUTURE

The exciting initiatives and ideas shared through this book can only truly succeed in engaging students when provided in conjunction with and supported by an extensive and vibrant information literacy education program in a library. These are part of a collaborative effort throughout libraries and across campuses to reach a goal of graduating information literate students. With programs and initiatives such as these and with librarians who are willing to continue to be creative and innovative in developing programming to engage undergraduate students, academic libraries will be thriving far into the future.

For color images, videos, and additional information related to this book and its chapters, please visit: http://publications.libraries.psu.edu/eresources/StudentEngagementandtheAcademicLibrary.

REFERENCE

Van Pelt, Peggy. "Putting Talent to Work in the Creation of the Learning Library." *Research Strategies.* 17, no. 2–3 (2000): 93–98.

1

Engaging Undergraduates with the Academic Library

Loanne Snavely, Head, Library Learning Services,
Penn State University Libraries

As librarians in academic libraries, engaging students with our libraries is our single most important imperative. Our first and highest priority needs to be educating our students to be lifelong information-literate learners. No matter how brilliant our collections or how perfect our services, if we are not engaging our students with those collections and services and with the scholarly information arena, we have failed as librarians and failed our institutions of higher education. Of course, we need to offer the best collections and services we can, but offering them is not enough; we must go a step further to ensure they are indeed used. We need to be victims of our own success; our libraries and resources should be used to capacity. Will they come? We cannot wait and see. Searching for ways to engage students with our information resources and providing the space and assistance to help them in integrating those resources with their learning to create new knowledge and to make meaning for themselves—these are the higher goals we must pursue. Through these goals, the library will truly be the heart of the university. This book and this chapter are an exploration of the creativity and innovation we need at this critical turning point in the history of libraries to engage students with the core of their education: taking advantage of knowledge gained over centuries, selecting what is interesting and relevant to themselves, and integrating all this into their own future and thus making their own meaning for themselves and for others. It is a big job, and at its best, it creates an excitement and sense of true confidence for students that will remain with them throughout their lives. Libraries are at a crossroads, and the academic library can thrive by claiming its place as a central and critical element in higher education by engaging students.

THE INFORMATION LITERACY CONTINUUM

Over the course of the past decade, innovative academic librarians have built on previous work and have added many elements to create dynamic programs that engage students at multiple levels, with the ultimate goal of achieving an information literate student body by graduation. A multitiered approach has become the framework for these efforts, including:

1. Initial engagement
2. First-level information literacy, including the introduction of library resources, research strategies, and information literacy concepts through a lower-division credit course or through course-related instruction and guest class presentations for first-level, hands-on introduction to library resources and databases in composition, speech communication, and ESL classes as well as web-based tutorials and online interactive multimedia learning objects
3. Upper-level, disciplinary information literacy, including upper-level disciplinary information research courses, course-related instruction within the disciplines, capstone courses and research methods courses; library liaison activities; and departmental and campus engagement
4. Graduate-level, in-depth specialized disciplinary research, graduate-level disciplinary research seminars, research methods courses, and individualized research consultations with subject specialist librarians

These tiers reflect the increasing depth of learning that would ideally be accomplished during higher education. They also reflect the idea of the "Information Literacy Continuum."

The Information Literacy Continuum really begins with the Literacy Continuum. Literacy is often defined, in part, by its opposite—illiteracy—and is usually meant to describe a very basic level of reading and writing ability—for example, the ability to read and understand a newspaper or to pass a literacy "test." Of course, we know a broad continuum of abilities exist in the reading and writing range, and we expect a very different level of reading comprehension and writing skills from an undergraduate at the college level than we do of a grade-school child. Information literacy is also a step in this continuum and assumes a level of basic literacy to succeed.

Within this framework, information literacy is itself a continuum, beginning with the skills that many—but not all—students gain in their K–12 curriculum and experience. While some schools have model information literacy programs, an increasing number of schools, including high schools, either have no library or have an outdated collection of books that has not been updated. Online resources also range from a substantial collection to none, so in some schools, teachers may encourage their students to find information on the open web. Libraries have been the brunt of budgetary crises, and many schools no longer fill their school librarian positions. Some students are now entering colleges and universities without the experience of a library or the use of an academically oriented collection, and the word *library* may only mean the collection of music on their iPod. Introducing students to a college or research library is becoming more critical to the initial engagement of students with libraries. This initial engagement requires effective activities to introduce the concept of libraries to incoming students who may have had little exposure to libraries—much less to a complex academic library—and to bridge the gap between the high school and college library experiences.

Engaging students through each of these tiers as they progress through their attainment of information literacy will become increasingly important as we look toward libraries' roles in the future.

FIRST IMPRESSIONS

The first tier, including the initial engagement, is essential to the success of the subsequent tiers and to overall student success. This initial engagement has been somewhat overlooked in recent years. After the general library orientation and tour went out of fashion in favor of more classroom and curriculum-related initiatives, the initial introduction to the library has not received the attention it deserves. In a research study on the first-year experience, we found that only a few librarians were creating truly innovative orientation-type activities (Cahoy and Snavely 2007), but the trend is growing. The idea that "first impressions" are long lasting holds as true for institutions such as libraries as it does for speed dating or career interviews, and librarians need to be very conscious of their libraries' first impressions on these teens who choose carefully where they will place their attentions and spend their time.

In order to create that positive first impression, a party has been hosted at all library locations at Penn State's University Park campus within the first few weeks of the fall semester for more than 10 years. An annual theme (luau, pirates, Mardi Gras, sports, PSU history, etc.) with accompanying decorations, great prizes and giveaways, and lots of publicity bring 3,500 to 5,000 students into the library each fall. The goals are to introduce students to the concept of a research library in a fun and informal way, to get them physically around to various subject libraries and service areas, and to make sure they know there are plenty of friendly faculty and staff to assist them with their information needs. Students are encouraged to come in groups with their friends, and many faculty members require the event for class assignment or extra credit, although more than half of the attendees come voluntarily at their own initiative. A certificate with locations serves as a guide upon entering, and each visited location is recorded with a stamp or a punch. Upon completion, this certificate is signed in the "prize room" and can be taken to class as proof of participation. Institutional Review Board–approved student surveys completed as they finish the event reveal an overwhelmingly positive attitude about the event, and 96 percent of students attending last fall felt that the Open House helped them learn more about the Libraries' many resources and physical spaces.

Interestingly, after years of hosting this event as an orientation and introduction type of activity intended to familiarize students with the "big picture" of the library and prepare them for the more in-depth information literacy learning activities they will be encountering, we discovered we were accomplishing other important library goals at the same time. *The University Libraries Marketing Steering Team: Final Report 2007–2008* provided an extensive exploration and examination of marketing issues through focus groups with students, class projects, and many additional sources. The team ultimately recommended the Open House as the Libraries' major marketing initiative for undergraduates. It was revealing to us that what began as a fun and upbeat learning activity also ended up promoting the library across campus. Recognizing this link between robust learning activities and promotion can be a rich area for us to attend to. Setting a tone of engaged learning and creating entry points for engaging students can then become its own energy for marketing. In our case, the Open House began creating a buzz around campus—not only with students but also with faculty and administrators who heard about it from students. Thus, the Open House has had a far reaching impact on campus, even to those who do not attend.

Institutions promote a range of activities to introduce the library, but examples such as simply hosting pizza in the library—a programming event one institution recently shared with me as their orientation activity—is not enough. Initial engagement events must have educationally purposeful goals, must introduce broad library concepts in a fun way, but must not try to teach resources or substitute for classroom activities. The trick is to not throw the "baby out with the bathwater"—that is, to not take the "basic library content" out of the event. It is a delicate balance to find the right approach for each individual institution, and many administrators have difficulty finding "fun in the library" as a worthwhile activity. Having acknowledged that, however, "fun in the library" combined with library and institutional learning goals can go a long way toward relieving anxiety, fostering a positive attitude, and introducing larger overall concepts that really set the stage and student readiness for the in-classroom activities that will follow. I think of these kinds of activities as "preinformation literacy" initiatives that meet affective and basic big picture goals and prepare students for success in the library classroom.

Another "first impression" issue is the role customer service plays in marketing and promoting the library. An unhappy incident involving poor customer service is repeated to friends and family far more frequently than a positive experience—and one negative experience requires multiple positive experiences to correct. We know that excellent service promotes the library, while poor face-to-face and virtual encounters detract from our image. Librarians and library staff cannot afford to offer poor service or poor service attitudes to their students. In spite of this, few libraries provide training for their staff on customer service. Ensuring that all library service providers are trained in basic customer service skills in addition to other library-related training will enable students and all library patrons to have positive, friendly, and courteous experiences as they use the physical and virtual library resources and services.

This is essential because students expect excellent customer service during all their encounters in life. Librarians who place a premium on customer service and on training their librarians and staff (including part-time and student staff) on providing excellent customer service at all service desks are more likely to see their students have a positive attitude toward the library and for students to come back to the library for assistance.

Another area to consider is that libraries have frequently been rule-based organizations, and finding a balance between enforcing rules and making our "customers" happy is challenging. Examining policies, fine structures, and other rules to see which ones are truly necessary and which can be made more flexible are part of helping to remove annoyances and confining restrictions as well as creating a positive attitude toward the library and its services.

Services also need to be available at the time and place students need them, even if it is in the wee hours of the morning. Building hours and virtual services should mirror the hours students are at work. Examining institutional data, such as tracking electronically the hours of computer usage and numbers of log-ons by location and time, will quickly identify student study and use patterns. These statistics begin to creep into the early morning hours after about the third week of the semester and continue to increase throughout the semester. Tracking use of physical spaces also shows a dramatic increase in late-night usage until the 24-hour area is a bustling beehive of activity after midnight during the last half of the semester. Even under tight economic conditions, libraries may find that keeping their doors open more hours has a huge positive impact. Staffing needs should be explored carefully and all issues examined. If 24/7 is not possible, 24/5 might be; if keeping the whole building open is not possible, keeping one area open may work through the addition of lockable doors or other strategies. Finally, students are often willing to accept few services in exchange for access to space, so reviewing and identifying the most essential and basic services will help pare down the number of staff needed.

As incoming students' attitudes, interests, and proclivities evolve over time, being sensitive and responsive to what engages them is an essential component of what librarians must do. Remember to begin at the very beginning, breaking down barriers and addressing affective aspects of engagement. Ultimately, you will wish to get on their radar, demonstrate the value of the library, and turn them into empowered information users so they will go into the workforce as capable and savvy information users. As students perceive information as easier to find, the Google generation is not an easy one to convince that library resources are needed or even useful. Therefore, the initial effort to engage these students is a critical first step in the academic libraries' continued long-range relevance and success.

INTRODUCING FUN THROUGH GAMES AND GAMING

Creating an element of fun can go a long way to lighten the atmosphere and enliven the activities related to introducing students to libraries and promoting comfort with a large research or academic library. Games and gaming have received a lot of attention in the past few years. Integrating library content and goals into games can assist in bringing the fun and the learning aspects of games into play. One of the reasons the Open House has been so successful is that it contains many fun and game-like elements. The overall structure is similar to a "big game" in the sense that students as "players" create their own strategies and find their way to many areas of the library, learning something at each location and verifying that they have accomplished that element through a stamp or hole punch in a map or certificate. In addition, many of the locations have game or game-like elements to help learn about them. For example, students are less aware than they used to be about what the humanities disciplines are. One year, in the Arts & Humanities Library, a croquet game was set up to play for prizes. Each wicket was labeled with a discipline related to that library, such as philosophy, religion, linguistics, history, literature, music, and art. As students played the game, they were reminded of the various subject areas they might encounter in that subject library as they hit their balls through the wickets. It was a simple, visual, and low-key way to reveal the disciplines represented in that subject library. Even students who chose not to play the game had a visual review as they visited that library. In another example, the Business Library had laptops set up with a *Jeopardy!*-like game featuring questions related to economics, finance, and world news. The Life Sciences Library often hosts a "nature trail" that guides students through the library, with stops at reference, current periodicals, and other points of interest. Special Collections hosts a "treasure hunt" in which students peruse the manuscripts, books, images, and other original materials in the exhibit cases to find answers to questions about the current exhibition.

These optional activities are designed to introduce information about the area in a fun way to participating students, who then also receive giveaways, roll dice for larger prizes, or enter a drawing to win larger prizes. Special prizes, such as a PSU T-shirt, for students who visit all library locations across campus have been very popular and have helped introduce the branch locations to more students. All students who complete the event can enter to win the grand prizes, which have included such items as iPads, laptops, and textbook scholarships (a semester's worth of free textbooks from a campus bookstore). In the open-ended survey questions, these gaming elements are often cited as favorite aspects of the Open House.

Creating games can be fun, challenging, and, at their grandest, expensive. The New York Public Library went all out in creating Find the Future, an all-night participatory game to celebrate the 100th anniversary of its famous library building. Participants from across the country wrote essays to compete to be one of the 500 players. The game highlighted 100 exciting famous and infamous objects and books from their collections, but players had to go one step further. Game designer Jane McGonigal tells players: "Find the Future is the first game in the world in which winning means writing a book." Throughout the night of the game and under heavy time constraints, players responded to prompts and wrote stories related to or inspired by the objects. These were collected and bound into a book during the course of the night that became part of the permanent New York Public Library collection. Being an author of a book archived forever in the collection helped create a feeling of ownership toward the library for a younger generation, which was one of the goals for the game (see http://www.nypl.org/audiovideo/find-future-nypl-game for more information).

There are a wide range of ways gaming and libraries can connect between this huge extravaganza and other simpler examples. Some libraries host game events and tournaments simply to bring students in. To really engage students with libraries, the association must be deeper and the integration clearer. Chapter 2 contains an example of a homegrown game that brings library learning goals together with a fun atmosphere to create an event that truly engages students.

CELEBRATING THE VISUAL

The visual aspects of our world are among our most important. Most people prize their eyesight and treasure whatever visual acuity they have above all other abilities. But the visual aspects of much of our academic content has been largely overlooked until fairly recently. Of course, in certain fields, such as art and architecture, it has been a primary medium; in others, such as medicine, the need for evaluating and recording X-rays and subsequent digital visual images have led the way for new developments and standards.

More recently, the visual component of our lives has taken on a new meaning as technology allows us to go beyond hearing another person on the phone to also seeing them. YouTube has revolutionized the home video arena, as has the iPhone's video capabilities. Google Images and Google Maps have increased manyfold the ease of access to images and visual geographical information. Technology has allowed the visual aspects of our lives to blossom through the ability to find and access still and moving images instantaneously, record them easily, and share them widely. Facebook and other sites have combined with mobile devices to enable the immediate sharing of something seen—from an amazing travel moment to a special wedding toast.

Just as various disciplines have created their own information literacy standards to capture the unique information habits and strategies unique to that discipline, the ideas related to visual information have been separated out of the "information equation" in order to highlight those unique qualities. Thus, even though visual information is one type of information—and as such is implicitly encompassed by information literacy and information literacy standards (http://www.ala.org/acrl/standards/informationliteracycompetency), which are by no means limited to text, as some have assumed—we have a new set of Visual Literacy Competency Standards (http://www.ala.org/acrl/standards/visualliteracy) that assist in focusing on the many unique aspects of visual information as we seek, find, evaluate, use and reuse it, and, of course, cite it appropriately!

Digital literacy, media literacy, and other terms are frequently in use to describe and name the activities surrounding the creation and use of media—most often, those involving still and/or moving images and sound. Students often prefer information delivered with visual and audio content and are increasingly invested in creating their own digital content. As multimedia becomes a regular part of everyone's daily lives, it also becomes an increasing part of the academic enterprise; therefore, academic libraries must turn their attention to not only accommodating but encouraging its use. Media Commons in a variety of forms—whether as part of an Information Commons or a Knowledge Commons or as a stand-alone initiative—are already part of many libraries and/or IT departments. An integration of technology and services is required because students need access to equipment and facilities for creating their own media as well as assistance in using the equipment and downloading and editing their video and sound recordings. The availability of such equipment and services for creation of video and digital content is as essential now as word processing once was—a basic and fundamental need rather than a special add-on need. But equipment and assistance with technology are only part of the equation.

When students create media projects, integrating library research materials into the information and resources they collect for these products is as relevant and essential as it is for the traditional research paper or presentation. Thus, integrating the library into these spaces needs to be more than just a lab existing in a library space. Students need assistance with scholarly and credible academic resources to draw on and incorporate into their media productions. Library resources—whether textual content from databases, image resources from newspaper archives or video content from television databases—are as important for a media project as they are for a research paper. Thus, the library can and should be an integral partner in any media initiative, and reference and research assistance should be as critical as other technical assistance for students. The library is also an important partner in discussions of copyright, fair use, and appropriate citation of sources used, regardless of format. Our new Knowledge Commons incorporates a media classroom with Macintosh computers and editing software so classes and workshops can include all aspects of media projects. The digital storytelling workshops that have been offered for several years as we have moved toward this model incorporate a component on finding scholarly and academic resources, including print, image, video, and sound, about copyright and fair use and about citing sources as well as on storyboarding, video editing, sound recording, and assembling the components of a media project. These workshops are cotaught by a librarian and a media technology specialist.

VISUAL ASPECTS OF LIBRARY SPACES

Visual impact and libraries have a broader aspect. As a place, the library has a visual and emotional impact on users as they enter. Librarians involved in building construction projects often struggle with the issues that architects raise as they try to accommodate library function while also producing a positive visual and emotional response by users. Ideally, the architects will accomplish both because libraries have a function in the life of the mind and imagination that a building can inspire as well as in the content their books and collections hold and can impart to their users. One library I feel excels in creating this ambiance is the new Lewis Science Library at Princeton University. It was clear during my visit that the visual impact of the building delighted the users and created an excitement within the space. This kind of excitement is something that can enhance the experience of any library user. The architects—Gehry Partners, LLP—have created amazing visual interest everywhere one looks (see http://www.arcspace.com/architects/gehry/princeton/princeton.html, http://www.princeton.edu/main/news/archive/S20/84/49I22/, http://thomasmayerarchive.de/categories.php?cat_id=1718&l=english). Bold colors, shadows, and the play of light awaken the senses and delight the eyes. Each space creates a special environment with a purpose in mind—whether it be browsing journal issues, working in groups, or finding a quiet space for immersing oneself in the process of gaining and creating knowledge. The emotional delight one can get from a physical space should not be overlooked in the affective aspect of creating an overall library experience.

The elegant and functional beauty of Virginia Tech's Architecture Library discussed in Chapter 12 is another space that engages users visually and physically in myriad ways. The expanse of glass that leads library users from the studio space on one side through the carefully designed commons space and then propels them visually into the grass and shade trees at the far end in one sweeping glance sets the tone for a great user experience. At its best, an architecture library can function as an extension of the architecture studio space, and this one does it superbly. The brilliant placement of the library entrance inside the architecture studio spaces means library users must first be immersed in the beehive of creative activity that an architecture studio space emits and then pass through that vibrant energy to reach the library. Once there, one is greeted by a visual landscape conducive to contemplation and imagination. The excellence of the total design concept and execution totally engages the students.

The new Knowledge Commons at Penn State, which was in the planning for many years and opened in January 2012, has been an instant success. The visual impact washes over the visitor as one enters. A "green wall" cascading with diverse plant species infuses the space with a lush feeling of clean air and creates a calm atmosphere. A multilevel and multifaceted ceiling of rich wood panels, interspersed with contemporary lighting, sets an exciting tone across the space. "Living rooms" with comfortable furniture are interspersed around the perimeter of the space, with high-tech collaborative group studies enclosed in glass DIRTT walls (http://www.dirtt.net), providing a sound barrier but keeping learning on display. Each collaborative space includes MediaScape capability and a large screen so all members of a group can connect their laptops, tablets, and/or iPads and alternate displays according to whose document or screen is the immediate topic of discussion. Whiteboards and the glass walls themselves are in frequent use as equations, chemical formulas, flow charts, drawings, lists and visual displays of all kinds flow across the surfaces. A small teaching space designed for intimate classes and consultations includes a couch surrounding a MediaScape connection and display with a bar behind the couch, allowing an intimate grouping for discussion and review—enabling multiple participants to share their work with the group and making learning visible. The center of the room is filled with student workstations—large enough for collaborative work but spaced to also enable individual work. Service areas are also seen immediately upon entering, offering library information and reference services, media, and technical assistance. Around the corner, the one-button glass studios allow students to record class presentations or practice their speeches with the click of a single button, removing barriers for the creative and learning processes. Cameras, audio-recording devices, lighting, and computers are already in place and ready to go. The resulting files are automatically saved to a jump drive that can be immediately taken to the adjacent editing studios. Finally, an innovative teaching and learning space designed to enhance learning through technology features four groups of Mac computers and multiple screens displaying images on all walls for a "surround" feel, enabling groups to work together, instructors to move easily throughout the class, and students to see clearly what is projected. The unique "in the round" design encourages innovative pedagogy and interaction between students and with instructors. Librarians and media staff teach in this room and also collaborate on digital storytelling workshops.

The adjacent Leisure Reading Room is filled with comfortable seating surrounded by low bookshelves containing best sellers, including the *New York Times* and other lists, graphic novels, popular fiction, and nonfiction. Seasonal displays (such as gardening for spring) and topical collections (such as cookbooks) are often featured. The books have been flying off the shelves. We are asked why an academic library would provide such a nonacademic collection. The reasons are numerous, but the conversations it invokes are enlightening. A faculty member thrilled by the collection observed that all reading informs a student's knowledge base and works its way into the overall education of the student. A writing tutor excited by the idea of the collection shared her belief that regular reading in an age of sound bites informs an understanding of structure and arguments. And we know that many students do not come to college with the sustained reading skills they need to excel. Practicing reading is the primary way to improve reading skills. Thus, a beautiful and comfortable room that invites students to stop and engage with books has been remarkably popular!

Creating desirable student spaces in previously unused or underutilized areas makes a lot of sense. With the increase in team projects and assignments in the curriculum, group study spaces are in increasing demand. At the University of Georgia, a series of group studies were added to a wide glass-walled bridge between buildings. These floor-to-ceiling glass cubicles allow those in the common areas to still see through the studies to the remarkable views of Atlanta out the windows and give the entire space an open and airy feeling. Demand for these areas is high, and an online reservation system enables students to sign up in advance, according to established guidelines.

Of course. not everyone can have exciting new creatively designed buildings or spaces, but any librarian can prepare arguments for campus administrators on why the library should have priority if an update is warranted. Each can think about ways of enhancing their spaces to give them visual appeal, even if it is in small ways and on a limited budget. It is definitely an area that should be given priority consideration if student engagement is a library goal.

One final note on creating visual excitement and community engagement is apparent at Syracuse University Library. Lesley Pease, head of the Learning Commons, has taken an innovative approach to providing visual interest in the library while also engaging students and bringing a new clientele into the library. In collaboration with a faculty member in the fiber arts program at the university, the library has become a show space for student artwork. The students, along with their instructor and a librarian, tour the library early in the semester, getting ideas for possible spaces and settings for a work of art. The students then propose installations of artwork for particular places, such as a window, a stairwell, an unused phone booth, or another area that appeals to them and that they find suitable for artwork they will create especially for those locations. The faculty member, a librarian, and the facilities staff all have the opportunity to review the proposals and locations for safety and other considerations before final installation takes place. These artworks add to the ambiance and visual interest of the library spaces—sometimes in surprising ways. Students who might not otherwise visit the library come in to see the artworks, just as they might in a gallery, and other students who might never venture into a gallery have the opportunity to see some original artwork created by their peers. At graduation time, family and friends also come in. In at least one case, a piece has been so successful as an artwork appropriate for the library and in its placement that the library has purchased the work and given it a permanent display location. Images of the artworks are shared through the "Fiber Arts" category on a Flickr site to document each year's works (http://www.flickr.com/photos/syracuse learningcommons).

CONCLUSION

Engaging students has many aspects—from first impressions and the creation of a fun and integrated introduction, through a variety of library connected educational practices, and finally into the visual, digital, and physical worlds of spaces and services for multimedia projects. Throughout all these, we must continually ask the question "How do students get engaged?" Librarians must continue to explore the answers for the library with the Information Literacy Continuum in mind.

As students change, the answers will change, but librarians must be constantly alert to the ever-changing landscape, exploring it and reaching out to meet its challenges. Students are engaged bit by bit—by a spark of interest, a new discovery, an interesting piece of information, a helpful librarian providing assistance, a project that connects them to their areas of interest, an internship that allows them to apply their emerging professional expertise to real problems, exciting spaces, and multimedia messages; these are some of the many ways students can be drawn into the fabric and meaning of the academic library.

Libraries will continue to change, and librarians must continue to explore new programs and initiatives. As long as there are libraries in institutions of higher education, engaging students will be the bottom line. If librarians focus their efforts in other directions and fail to engage students, they will indeed be in trouble, as the many predictions in the media call out for the extinction of libraries. Creative librarians will track students needs' and find innovative ways to engage them with the library enterprise.

REFERENCE

Cahoy, Ellysa Stern, and Loanne Snavely. "Engaging First-Year Students: Developing Library-Related Cocurricular Activities That Impact and Empower Students." In *The Role of the Library in the First College Year*, edited by Larry Hardesty, 122–135. Columbia, SC: National Resource Center for the First-Year Experience and Students in Transition, 2007.

2

Using an Alternate Reality Game to Engage Students in Learning

Emily Rimland, Information Literacy Librarian,
Penn State University Libraries

Suddenly, the university's one-of-a-kind mascot disappears. Who is behind the caper? At first blush, this may sound like some college-age pranksters at work or a rival team up to no good, but really, it is a new type of learning in action. It is not news that games for educational purposes are a rapidly expanding area of interest and research. Within this newfound area, different types of games are being developed and explored for specific purposes and settings. Alternate reality games (ARGs) are a particular type of game that started in the commercial world and have recently debuted in education. This chapter will explain what ARGs are and how they can be employed as educational tools, and I will provide a specific example of how an ARG worked in a library setting and strategies to consider when developing this type of game.

WHAT ARE ARGS?

Virtual reality, *augmented reality*, and *alternate reality* are among the many terms that describe some other type of actuality aside from the one in which we are currently present. Not to be confused with similar-sounding terms, ARGs offer a new approach that allows educators to rethink and reshape traditional learning—all of which happens in real life but with a twist.

The main goal behind ARGs is to pique the gamers' curiosity and interest so much that at some point, they question what is real and what is part of the game. This feeling can be attributed to the fact that ARGs pull together real-world events, places, and items along with virtual ones. ARGs typically have a finite time period where they are active and usually kick off with some type of out-of-the-ordinary event. This event—often referred to as a rabbit hole (a nod to the event that got Alice's adventure started)—can be anything from the chimerical to ordinary but is typically something just odd enough to get curious folks interested. After players enter the game via the rabbit hole, their interest is sustained by a variety of cryptic clues or quests that lead them through the game. In the end, players feel like they have had a shared experience with other players, the game master, or actors in the game. Generally, an ARG results in some type of reward, which can be anything from a grand prize to the satisfaction of achievement, participation, and completion.

ARGs in some shape or form have been around since the 1990s but got their notoriety through the commercial sector, specifically marketing. Because of their roots in marketing, many ARGs are associated with specific products. The first well-known, mainstream ARG is credited to one called "The Beast," which was a promotion for the release of the Steven Spielberg movie *A.I. Artificial Intelligence* in 2001. Next came one by Microsoft called "I Love Bees" in conjunction with the launch of the new *Halo 2* video game (Borland, 2005, p. 2). Another famous ARG is "Year Zero," related to the release of an album by the musical group Nine Inch Nails. Many ARGs are associated with entertainment because they are a way to get fans to interact, to hype them up before a release, to spread the word to friends, and to also scour advertisements for clues. ARGs of this scale are often extremely tricky to the point where players are forced to collaborate to decipher the clues, but the results are worth it—often leading to special prizes, such as being the first to play the game or to get a special screening of a film.

You may be thinking ARGs sounds similar to scavenger hunts or web quests, and ARGs do indeed have elements of both of these, but ideally, ARGs are a blend of both, which creates a new genre. Nor are ARGs video games, "though electronic devices-including computers, cell phones, and GPS-enabled handhelds—are frequently used to access clues. ARGs are not role-playing games, in that players generally function as themselves in a real-world environment" (EDUCAUSE, 2009, p. 1). Additionally, ARGs capitalize on the players' intrinsic interest to creatively solve problems, use technology, and discover their environment. No list of step-by-step instructions tells what to do in an ARG. Rather, there are typically multiple ways to get to the "end" of the ARG, and in some games, not all clues may be uncovered by every player. These principles are also true for the game's developers (also known as puppet masters), who have endless ways to pose critical thinking situations. Alternate reality games should be a source for innovative instructional design by using technology, collaboration, and out-of-the-box creativity.

USING ARGS AS LEARNING AND ENGAGEMENT TOOLS

ARGs have provided a platform for the commercial sector to get fans involved with its products on a deeper level, but more recently, higher education has adopted ARGs as an imaginative way to help students learn. Not only do ARGs encourage the use of a variety of resources, such as the open web, scholarly research, library collections, and multimedia, but they also encourage collaboration and groupthink. In short, they are a dynamic way to introduce resources and services to students and have the students put their problem-solving and critical thinking skills to the test.

Librarians have a unique role because of the wide breadth and depth of resources and services they offer to their communities. Because these resources are easily accessible to the game's developers and library employees have a wide and deep knowledge of them, they are some of the best people to create an ARG.

Libraries as a community hub are another reason they can uniquely play host to an ARG. What better place to use the tools often associated with ARGs than a library? In a library, the items players will likely need are housed under one roof, they are found in a space many know and use already, and players have access to help in many forms. ARGs also lend themselves well to helping students develop targeted research skills and techniques they will use as scholars and professionals, thus promoting the library's role in lifelong learning. By problem solving their way through the game, students are engaging in activities that more closely emulate real-world tasks than traditional classrooms provide; therefore, ARGs allow for the opportunity to reach students who may not visit the library for course-related instruction or the type of learner who does not respond to traditional pedagogy.

CREATING AN ARG

When I came across EDUCAUSE's "7 Things to Know About Alternate Reality Games in 2009," the concept of an ARG was immediately intriguing. Penn State University librarians are always on the lookout for new and creative ways to involve students and get them interested in what the libraries have to offer. This is easier at Penn State because a successful annual event called the Libraries' Open House is already in place and consistently draws more than 3,500 students each year. The Open House was initiated 10 years ago as a means to relieve students' library anxiety, especially in their first year at the university. This self-guided tour of the libraries' physical spaces provides students with a party-like atmosphere for learning about our services and an opportunity to interact with friendly staff. Students also have the chance to win a handful of grand prizes at the Open House, which over the past years have included textbook scholarships, laptops, and iPads.

Although the Open House was created to be a big picture introduction to the libraries, in the assessment of the event via surveys, students asked for more in-depth opportunities to learn about library resources at the event. The ARG was conceived as an add-on to the Open House as one answer to this need for a deeper experience for some students. It was also a dynamic way for anybody to learn about the libraries' resources and services and an opportunity to try creating new ways of learning.

Once the idea to create an ARG was approved by the Open House team leaders, the real work of creating the game began. At this time, it was possible to secure a motivating prize for one lucky ARG player—a Dell laptop—which was critical for getting students to play and sustain motivation. Players who completed the game would be entered into a drawing for the laptop. Also, the first 100 players were given an Open House T-shirt as a prize for finishing the ARG.

The toughest and yet the most exciting part of creating an ARG is developing the overall game flow and clues. Because ARGs typically involve a narrative that wraps around the game and gives it structure and context, this is where to begin development. Interested parties were invited from the libraries as well as the campus's Media Commons and Educational Gaming Commons to participate in the initial brainstorming session. During this session, many great ideas were gathered, and it was possible to begin focusing the direction, reviewing successful initiatives, and exploring lots of possibilities for the direction of the ARG. After this "spitballing" session, a core group of four members formed the ARG development team.

At the brainstorming session. focus was placed on the specific skills and outcomes ARG participants would have upon completion of the game. Open House surveys pointed out that many students wanted to leave the Open House with a deeper knowledge of library services and resources. This was very helpful to librarians, who had a good understanding of the student undergraduate population and who knew what kinds of information literacy skills are needed. With this in mind, learning outcomes for the ARG are:

At the completion of the ARG, students will be able to:

- Effectively search the library's catalog (the CAT) in order to find a specific book and then navigate to that area of the library by using a Library of Congress call number.
- Use a library database and the basics of constructing a search strategy in order to find a specific article.
- Become familiar with a digitized collection and employ one of the available formats (online, microfilm, and print) to answer the quest.

The initial brainstorming group also worked hard to establish narrative and rabbit hole ideas. After a lively discussion, the group decided to maximize two unique things about the library and the campus in our narrative: the last remaining specimen of the school mascot (the Nittany Lion), which resided in the library, and a university president who was an amateur magician. These two things led to the basic premise: The original Nittany Lion goes missing because of a botched magic trick by the president. The students' job is to uncover the clues that will help reverse the spell in order to return the lion to its home in the library. Because the Nittany Lion was on display in the lobby of one of the main entrances to the library, this provided an easy rabbit hole due to its high visibility to patrons entering the library.

Once the rabbit hole idea was solidified, the next step was to provide the narrative and background to the players as to why the Nittany Lion went missing in order to pull them deeper into the game. It was at this point that some cross-campus collaboration was drawn with Penn State Media Commons. The Penn State Media Commons serves as a means to help the Penn State community create, produce, and publish multimedia projects. Because members from this group attended the initial brainstorming session, their early participation in the project resulted in their help in creating a professional video to quickly explain the backstory of the missing Nittany Lion.

It also helped that the university president loved to perform and agreed to star in the film. This in turn helped to convince the libraries' dean to also provide a cameo appearance in the video—all of which made it more exciting for developers and players. In fact, in a final survey of ARG participants, the video (which you can see at http://vimeo.com/6548882) was frequently named as players' favorite part of the game! At the close of the video, players are charged with their task:

Your mission should you choose to accept it, is to follow the clues and puzzles to discover how to bring the Nittany Lion back to Pattee Library. Complete three quests along the way, each one unlocking a clue to the next quest as well as helping you to build a final enchantment that breaks Dr. Spanier's spell. Good luck!

This left the question of how to get potential players to the video online because the Nittany Lion disappeared in real life and the issue of someone not seeing that the lion was missing if they did not happen to walk by it the week that the game was active. This issue was solved by creating a customized word search puzzle that was printed and distributed at several locations in the library, in classes, and also through the student newspaper, *The Daily Collegian*. Players had to find all the words in the puzzle, which did not in itself give the answer but required some additional puzzling to get to the URL for the video (see Figure 2.1).

Once outcomes, the basic premise, the rabbit hole, and the video were taken care of, the development group moved on to creating an overall storyboard and framework for the game. This proved to be very challenging yet rewarding to see all the pieces eventually come together to form the game. The team realized early on that it would need to provide some type of safety net or home base for the players in the event that something went wrong with a clue, a player got confused, or players wanted to communicate with other players. Luckily, the university provided the solutions to these questions once again.

First, the university provides a virtual hosting service that allowed the creation of a separate website outside of the libraries' main site, which gave more flexibility in terms of website design and layout. Once the new site was in place, the university's blog software was installed on the site (Movable Type). The blog software was critical in providing a safety net primarily because the commenting feature allowed gamers to leave feedback at different stages, thereby communicating with the developers and other players. Indeed, the blog platform proved very useful for these purposes. For example, a copy of a fake book (a box disguised to look like a book) that gamers needed to find got misshelved (either accidently or on purpose). A player alerted us via a comment, and we were quickly able to locate and reshelve the missing clue. Additionally, players left comments that told how they were doing or what they thought of the game (e.g., "OK. I finally found the answer for this clue. Dell, I'm coming!!!"). Essentially, this site was used as a home base throughout the game. As players solved each "quest," they were led to a new URL on the home base for subsequent clues. Additionally, the site was used for entering the final answer and pointing participants to the survey and prize drawing.

From this point, the game developers created three quests, which were tied to the main objectives and learning outcomes. These quests employed targeted research tools and techniques that students need as scholars and, later, as professionals.

The following paragraphs will take you briefly through the ARG's storyline. Gamers started with the rabbit hole of seeing the Nittany Lion "missing" (i.e., covered up by a large display) while attending the libraries' Open House or throughout the entire week that the game was active (see Figure 2.2).

It is very important that you consult with stakeholders before doing something this dramatic. Before we covered the lion, administration had to sign off on the plan and we had to work closely with the Preservation Department to create and print the massive poster that completely covered the Nittany Lion diorama.

Players could enter the game through a variety of venues. When they saw the missing lion, they were able to take a printed puzzle at this location. Printed puzzles were also distributed at other locations during the Open House and before some library classes. Another possible entry point was the same puzzle printed *in The Daily Collegian*. All these ways led players to the game's website, where they viewed the video and got their next clue to continue.

The first "in game" quest involved a plea to help bring back the lion, with the hint that a clue might be found in the libraries' collection in a particular book about magic

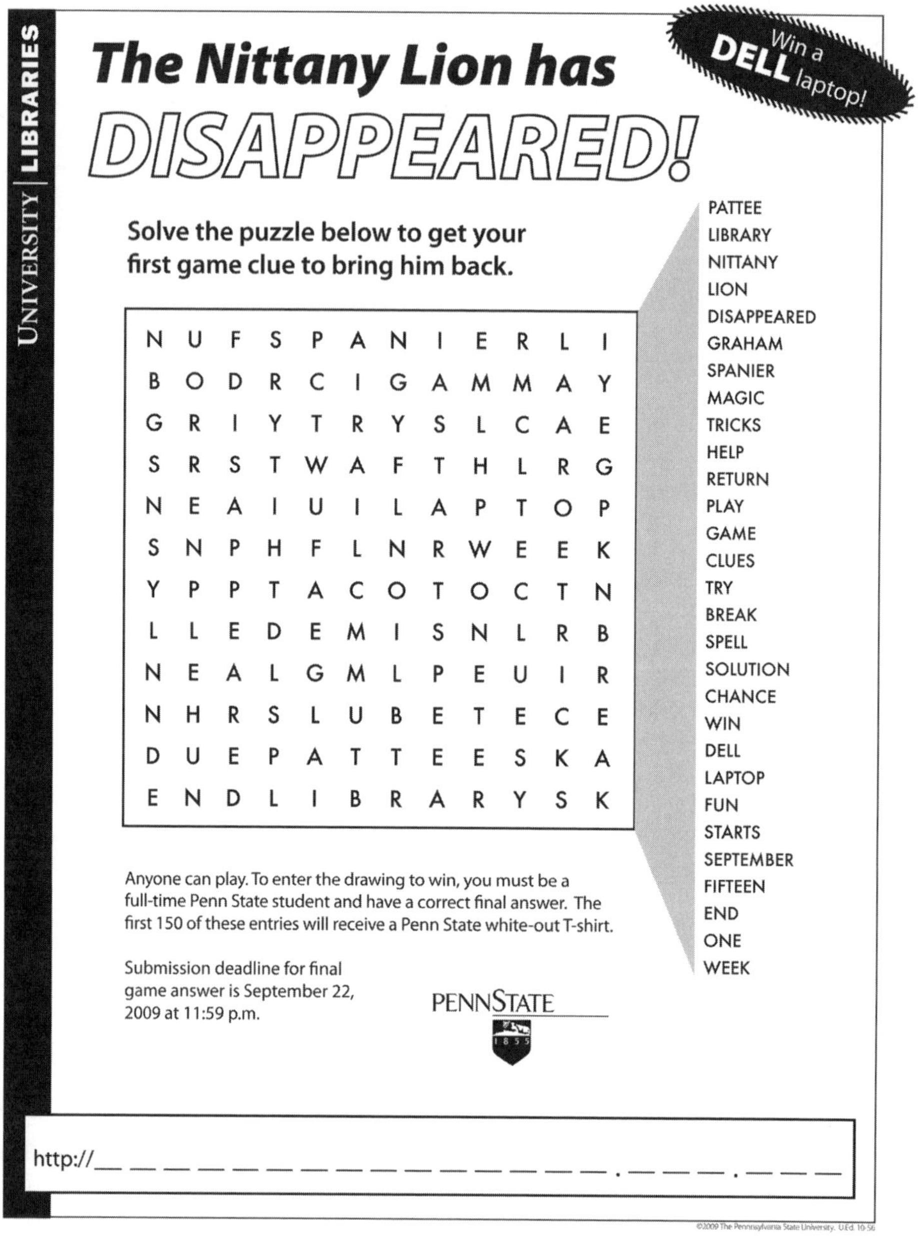

Figure 2.1 This puzzle leads participants to the first clue. The source of inspiration for this puzzle was one of the MIT Libraries' Puzzle Challenges, which also sought to teach students about library resources (http://libraries.mit.edu/about/puzzle/archive.html)

Figure 2.2 The Nittany Lion mascot display was covered by this large poster to capture potential players' attention (also known as "the rabbit hole") and direct them to the first puzzle (shown in Figure 2.1).

tricks gone horribly wrong. A record was created in the online catalog for a book with a similar title, and copies were available in two locations in the library: one in the appropriate subject library and one in the reserves room. The clue was attached in the details part of this record in the online catalog in the event someone would stumble upon the record and get pulled into the ARG this way (another entry point). Having two copies of the fake book gave gamers some choice as to which copy they located, allowing them to explore different parts of the library. It also allowed the placement of one copy in the extended hours area of the library (open 24 hours a day, 5 days a week) so the game could be played at almost any time. The books placed on the shelves were actually boxes disguised as books and opened to offer the next clue on slips of paper: a cryptic message that when decoded resulted in a single word. This word was once again used to build a new URL, at which the next task awaited.

Back at the ARG website, the next quest involved using a general periodical database to pull up a particular newspaper article that contained a quote about the library by then football coach Joe Paterno. Gamers used a word from this quote to build another URL to move on to the next clue. Ideally, in this quest, gamers found the specific database and worked out a search strategy to arrive at the correct article to find the quote. However, from feedback, it was learned that a handful of students were able to Google to find the answer. Although googling was actually a more time-consuming approach for the gamer, it still probably taught them about using keywords and search strategies to get different search results. The survey also showed that this was the most challenging quest for many.

The last quest involved the use of Sanborn Fire Insurance maps from 1911. Gamers used another clue to locate the original Carnegie Library on the Penn State University Park campus on the map and had the choice of using the maps online, in microform, or in print. By all accounts, all formats were used, although the online version of the map was the most popular. After completing this last part, players had completed three quests and had one final piece to complete. This last piece involved using the first three clues and a final word to fill in the blanks to complete the reversal "spell" that would return the Nittany Lion to its rightful home:

In his _____ to Penn State,
For her founders strong and great,
Fred _____ poured out his _____,
So our lion now stands guard;
For the _____ of Old State,
Brave mascot resume your fate.

This last piece to the puzzle—checking answers and entering participants for the prize drawing—was managed by a program developed in-house that autochecked the answers for accuracy as well as the status of the player. Faculty and staff were invited to play the ARG but were not eligible to win prizes. Students had to be currently enrolled but could be undergraduate or graduate status. The in-house program first verified that the final answers were correct and then asked the person to enter his or her PSU access account. The program then looked up the students' information and confirmed that they were an enrolled student and had not already entered the prize drawing. If the system was able to verify all these things, the participant was taken to a survey that entered them into the grand prize drawing and recorded his or her T-shirt size. At the close of the ARG, which was open for one week, we had 661 unique visits to the game website and 583 views of the video trailer. A total of 119 gamers completed the game, of which 109 were students and 10 were faculty or staff. Without having done anything like this before, we were quite pleased with this outcome and considered it an instant success.

ARG OUTCOMES AND ASSESSMENT

Because the ARG was a brand-new activity for the library, we felt strongly that it was important to be able to assess it as a learning tool and the overall satisfaction on the part of the gamers. Once gamers completed the game and entered into the prize drawing, they had the option to complete our survey, and all but a few people chose to complete it. (Note: IRB guidelines prohibit researchers from requiring participants to complete the survey in order to get their prize; rather, the survey must be voluntary.)

From the ARG survey, 96 percent of respondents strongly agreed or agreed that the ARG helped them learn more about Penn State University Libraries. Perhaps even more telling was the fact that 100 percent of respondents strongly agreed or agreed that they would play a similar game again. Respondents were also asked for feedback about their favorite parts of the game, the most challenging part, and the easiest part, to which we received a variety of answers. The fact that there was much diversity in responses to these questions was satisfying to the game developers because it signified that a good balance of questions was provided for different types of learners. Not one thing was too hard or too easy. Similarly, gamers cited liking different parts of the game. Although not much is known about how long it took gamers to complete the game, it took the game testers about 45 minutes to complete the game and the first real gamers finished about an hour after the game went live. Some took considerably longer to finish, but players had up to a week to complete the game if they chose to pace themselves.

Deciphering when and where gamers got frustrated or lost interest in the game was more difficult. Once again, the Google Analytics for the site counted 661 unique visits after the launch of the ARG and 583 people viewed the video trailer, so obviously many people started the game and/or viewed the video and chose not to play the game or played only part of the game. While a few top-performing players may have finished the game quickly, the quests may have been dauntingly difficult for many who tried. One lesson learned was to try and track these potential players more closely and try to determine when and why they drop out, as well as explore ways to keep them progressing in the game.

Lastly, the survey asked respondents for any general feedback about the ARG, and it was delightful to read overwhelmingly positive responses about the game. A few selected positive comments include:

- "The feel of a game in the real world where I have to interact with things from reality to finish the game."
- "It was difficult. Needs to be even more challenging."
- "Overall, it was a great learning experience that my friends and I enjoyed a lot!"
- "Overall, this was a fantastic game. I hope I win the laptop or shirt, but either way, the experience was loads of fun!"
- "Challenging and fun at the same time."
- "This game was the best thing of my day."
- "I would love that this game involved more than just a library, but a campus wide hunt. Like going to historical places or new places with historical facts about the university."
- "It was awesome and intense."
- "It was a fun activity and I would do it again. Since my major is education, I can integrate similar ideas into my classroom for projects."

This last comment was especially pleasant to read because it speaks to the transfer of knowledge from the game developers to the learner. In this case, education students might be more likely to employ games in their careers as teachers because they experienced a game firsthand and had a favorable experience. This idea of teaching future teachers by way of example is yet another benefit of educational games.

Other feedback was generally constructive and cited particular parts that gamers found unclear or difficult:

- "Searching the database was a little unclear."
- "I would suggest to expand the game, maybe add more quests."
- "Also it would help if the players could interact with people too."
- "Maybe through telephone, e-mail or instant messaging (AIM) to deepen the feeling of an Alternate reality game."
- "I liked it but it was during my studies for exams which is bad."
- "There were a couple times where I was felt snagged, but was mostly a mistake of user-error. . . . Just be mindful of some of the minor issues that can arise due to user-error."

Most of the difficulty mentioned in the feedback that pertained to particular clues or quests resulted from clue language or how the player interpreted a clue. By nature of purposefully creating cryptic clues, the game developers knew they were running this risk of creating some confusion but accepted this as par for the course. Having the blog site as a safety net also allowed creators to feel more comfortable with any ambiguity in the game because players had a way to provide feedback. A few comments on the blog of this nature allowed interjecting hints or encouragement to help players.

As we reflected on the ARG postgame survey results and our learning outcomes created at the onset of the game, the ARG results aligned closely with our objectives. It was pleasing that players finished with more knowledge about the libraries and had fun along the way.

LESSONS LEARNED AND WHAT TO CONSIDER WHEN DEVELOPING AN ARG

While the ARG had many positive outcomes, other things could be changed or done differently. One proactive step that should definitely be repeated is to have student testers conduct dry runs of the game. Because of the collaboration with the Educational Gaming Commons, it was possible to enlist an undergraduate student tester who had an interest in educational gaming as well as a graduate student who was a part-time library employee who also had an interest in this field. Both testers tried the game without any insider knowledge or hints and were therefore able to provide objective criticism of the game. This criticism led us to change a few small things that were problematic or unclear to the testers, and it had a positive result to have taken this step.

The area of development that caused most to struggle was finding and knowing when one had achieved the appropriate level of difficulty. The developers felt much like Goldilocks, trying to find porridge that was "just right" for the students. If it were too difficult, it would dissuade them from pressing forward; conversely, if it were too easy, it would not maintain their interest or teach new skills. In the end, the feedback pointed out that the ARG should have been made somewhat more challenging. Because many who did not complete the game did not give feedback, it may have indicated a higher degree of difficulty for those who began the game but did not finish it. Overall, this first try was considered to be highly satisfactory.

Knowing your audience and outlining your outcomes prior to game development is key to developing an ARG. While in the throes of development, you may find yourself "in the weeds," getting bogged down with details or strategies. Having the outcomes for your particular setting clearly stated ahead a time will serve as a very strong rudder to keep everyone focused on what is important.

ARGs lend themselves beautifully to collaborations with campus partners. Use them as an opportunity to work with groups you would like to connect with or as a way to learn new skills for yourself (e.g., video production). In the end, you will have a better, more diverse game and stronger partnerships as a result of reaching out to constituents.

Look at other genres of games and other ARGs for ideas and consider consulting with a puzzle master. If creating an ARG is something outside your bailiwick, find people who have an interest in ARGs or other types of games for your development team. If you have the resources, consult with a puzzle or game master to help with the game's structure and strategies. If nothing else, having creative thinkers who are eager to help create an ARG will go a long way toward creating a stimulating game.

Lastly, get the support of your administration and team before you start an ARG. You will need time, resources, and people to help you pull it off and getting buy-in from a broad array of colleagues will help you accomplish your goals.

FUTURE PLANS FOR THE ARG

One limitation of the ARG that was recognized early on but not easily rectified was the fact that it was only available to students at the University Park campus. This meant that neither the other Penn State campuses nor distance learners could participate; therefore, plans for the ARG are to make it a completely online game so all students can play if they wish. Another future change will be to make the game almost completely self-sustaining so it does not need to be monitored very closely. Students could play as they see fit and have the time. Naturally, these changes will require some restructuring of the game, but, hopefully, some elements can remain the same, as can the overall narrative. Additionally, other changes, such as a new dean and a new home for the Nittany Lion, have added an element of "unreality" to the game. Whether the ARG video might need to be reshot or edited in some way or might be left as part of the "alternate reality" elements of the ARG is still under discussion.

One challenge of the online format will be how to reward players. Obviously, it will not be possible to offer laptops or T-shirts as prizes on a regular basis, so a big question is what would work as an incentive. Additionally, the game could become something instructors may want to assign as part of a class, so what proof could be offered that students completed the game on their own? These are new questions presented by the online-only format, which must be negotiated. However, the idea of being able to offer this learning tool to a broader audience is incentive enough for the developers to discover a way to make the ARG work in a new way.

ARGs offer new and exciting ways to engage students and help them to expand their information literacy skills. ARGs also offer opportunities for librarians to develop instructional techniques that teach learners in unconventional ways. Although ARGs require intense planning and sustained creativity, the reward of witnessing energetic learners who crave and ask for more is well worth the effort.

REFERENCES

Borland, John. "Blurring the Line between Games and Life." *CNET News* (2005). http://news.cnet.com/Blurring-the-line-between-games-and-life/2100-1024_3-5590956.html?tag=mncol;1n.

EDUCAUSE. "7 Things You Should Know About . . . Alternate Reality Games." (2009). http://net.educause.edu/ir/library/pdf/ELI7045.pdf.

3

Lost in the Stacks: The Research Library Rock 'n' Roll Radio Show!

Ameet Doshi, Head, User Experience Librarian and Assessment Coordinator, Georgia Institute of Technology Library

"The library on the radio? How would that work?" That very question was asked while brainstorming possibilities for connecting the library with Georgia Tech students outside the library. It turns out the answer surprised both librarians: a weekly radio program that mixes library talk and music.

In January 2010, the library's East Commons coordinator, Charlie Bennett, and I worked with Georgia Tech undergraduate and graduate students to launch the research library rock 'n' roll radio show on WREK 91.1 FM in Atlanta, founded in 1968 and operated and funded entirely by students and the Student Government Association, respectively. This may be the first and only such program dedicated to research libraries, although hopefully other academic librarians will be inspired by this project and start programs of their own.

IN THE BEGINNING

This unique collaboration between the library and student radio began as an attempt to market library events and resources via brief one- to two-minute public service announcements on WREK. After doing some "blue sky" brainstorming, this small nugget of a library outreach project eventually turned into a proposal for a weekly hour-long radio program. The radio show is called *Lost in the Stacks* and broadcasts live at noon every Friday. The show is a mix of interviews with students, faculty, and library staff about a library-related theme interspersed with theme-related music.

Adapted from Robert Fox, Cathy Carpenter, and Ameet Doshi. "Cool Collaborations: Designing a Better Library Experience." *College & Undergraduate Libraries* 18 no. 2–3 (2011): 213–227. Portions reprinted by permission of the publisher (Taylor & Francis Ltd., http://www.tandfonline.com).

For example, a show with the theme "The Library and Film" included interviews with the librarian responsible for developing the library's film collection, undergraduate students from the film club about how they use the library as a setting for many of their films, and a Georgia Tech faculty member about her use of the library's scholarly film resources. Each interview is divided up by a set of theme-related music. Keeping with the example of "The Library and Film," music sets included songs about films or related to the process of filmmaking (for example, "Clark Gable" by The Postal Service and "Favorite Films" by Television Personalities). Other themes explored on *Lost in the Stacks* include:

- "Maps and Legends"
- "Building"
- "Science Fiction"
- "Women's History"
- "Living a Life of the Mind"
- "Finals Stress and the Library"
- "The Library at Night"
- "Academic Freedom and Libraries"
- "Books: Past, Present, and Future"
- "Old [Library] Technologies"
- "Oceanography"
- "Computers and Libraries"
- "Conspiracy Theories: Separating Fact from Fiction"
- "The Library and Academic Success"
- "Library Instruction"
- "Bookmaking"
- "Library Design"
- "Art Libraries"
- "Libraries and the News Media"
- "Student Scholarly Communication"
- "Libraries in Other Lands"

A complete list of programs is available by visiting the *Lost in the Stacks* Facebook page at http://www.facebook.com/LostIntheStacks. Furthermore, set lists for songs played on each show are also available via this website.

THE PROCESS

The process of obtaining a regular slot on the weekly rotation involved communication within the library as well as with the student leadership of the station. The hosts were first asked to submit a written proposal about the program to WREK and then record a pilot episode for evaluation by the WREK executive board. Fortunately, a number of students indicated an interest in the idea and offered their production skills to help record the first pilot episode and serve as board operators each week. Every program on WREK requires a student board operator controlling the technical aspects of the show, and many students sit in on the show each week to offer their opinions and ideas about libraries. Some of the on-air conversations between the WREK students and library staff often include such phrases as "I had no idea that the library did that!"

or "Wow, I definitely need to check that [resource, service, collection] out!" The fact that such conversations about the library are happening "live" and broadcast over the airwaves gives listeners a sense of authenticity about the breadth of serendipitous encounters possible between library users and library staff.

Some of the most powerful conversations on *Lost in the Stacks* have taken place between a librarian, a student, and a faculty member. For example, during a show about conspiracy theories, the faculty member teaching a course on the subject discussed his thoughts about fact checking with two students from his class who were also in the studio. In addition, the librarian for that discipline shared her ideas and approaches for fact checking. This is an example of when aspirations for an engaging, discussion-oriented library radio show actually turned into reality.

Because student schedules can be erratic, it was necessary to recruit three or four backup student operators who would be willing and able to step in at the last minute if needed. Producing each week's show involves two to three hours of research, scheduling guests, recording interviews, and racking our musical histories to come up with 30 minutes worth of theme-related music.

MARKETING

To help market the program, a URL was purchased and a simple website (http://lostinthestacks.org) was created. This directs users to the Facebook page, which was simple to set up and effective in creating an interactive conversation among audience members. In addition, the Facebook page is intentionally designed to allow non-Facebook users the ability to see pictures, click links, and see the set lists for each show. As of April 2012, the site has more than 650 fans, many of whom actively communicate their thoughts about *Lost in the Stacks* on the Facebook wall. Some comments include:

- "Thanks for having me on the show! It was a blast!"
- "Thanks for including my song!!"
- "Awesome show today—really liked the theme and you guys played Morphine! (and my fave R.E.M. song)."
- "Something to explore: postliterature."
- "This is amazing!!!"
- "OK, that's weird. Just 60 seconds ago, I was telling someone here how great Seattle's Central Library was."
- "Even in my dreams at night, I would find myself in the library—that's how much it meant to me."

Not surprisingly, a large portion of the Facebook fans (and, presumably, listeners) are Georgia Tech undergraduate students. The show is available for one week on the WREK webpage, and many of the interviews are also archived in podcast format in SMARTech, the library's institutional repository. In addition to the Facebook page, the *Lost in the Stacks* Twitter feed (@libraryradio) was launched. The Twitter feed has been a useful supplement to the Facebook page, and some of the student assistants and fans of the show will tweet comments during the program by using the #LostintheStacks hash tag.

Although it is not currently possible to accurately determine how many listeners are tuned in via radio or how many are tuned into the archive, it is possible to count the number of "live stream" listeners. Given the sheer size of the metro Atlanta area and the fact that the WREK signal presently reaches a roughly a 50-mile radius, it is entirely possible that many of these listeners are in their cars driving to lunch on a Friday afternoon. Periodically, they call into the station—usually one or two per show—complimenting either the music selections or the interviews or both. The station normally gives out tickets to upcoming area concerts, and on rare occasions, listeners are asked to call in to the studio to win concert tickets.

BROADCASTING, STREAMING, AND PODCASTING

College and public radio stations should possess a license from the Federal Communications Commission (FCC) to broadcast music and other programming over the airwaves. Thus, specialty shows, such as *Lost in the Stacks*, operate under a standard "umbrella" license for broadcast on the air. In addition to the FCC license, many public and college radio stations also obtain a separate license to stream online as well as stream an archive of copyrighted music for a limited period of time (typically, one or two weeks) on their website. The policies for broadcast and online streaming are determined at the station management level and are quite standard across the industry, so specialty hosts normally do not need to be concerned with licensing issues. However, if the goal is to *podcast* copyrighted music, then it is important to obtain guidance regarding the process from legal counsel at the radio station or university. Indeed, a future goal for the *Lost in the Stacks* program is to distribute the entire show, including the copyrighted music, via a downloadable podcast. But as noted, because of the copyright issues involved, such distribution via podcast will require additional research and resources before it becomes a reality. In the meantime, the archive of the program is streamed via the WREK website as permitted by the license obtained by WREK station management (available at http://wrek.org/lostinthestacks).

Even without being in podcast format, the show has garnered attention within the library community as well as among students and faculty at Georgia Tech. Listener evaluations suggest that the radio program has been a successful, low-cost, high-impact collaboration with student media that helps shape user perceptions of the Georgia Tech library and library staff in new and positive ways.

The show does involve some monetary cost because music is obtained for the program by staff, usually via iTunes or Amazon. Currently, no financial cost is charged to the library other than the commitment of staff time by the two cohosts. However, this commitment of time is not insignificant. Any unique collaboration that involves scheduling time for interviews and meetings can take hours out of the standard work week. Fortunately, the library's administration has been entirely supportive of this outreach activity. The collaboration leverages existing infrastructure and uses existing marketing channels (such as Facebook and Twitter) to gain listeners. It is important to note that although *Lost in the Stacks* may be the first such library radio program, the program will hopefully encourage other academic librarians to engage their users in similarly unique and fun ways.

ACCESSIBLE AQUARIUM PROJECT

In the spring and summer of 2010, the library collaborated with Georgia Tech's Center for Assistive Technology and Environmental Access (CATEA) to house a "virtual aquarium" project within the library space. The goal of the virtual aquarium project is to make the aquarium and other museum experiences more accessible—in this case, for the visually impaired.

Using a video camera that applies metadata to moving objects, the technology identifies and tracks different species of fish and then assigns a musical instrument to each species. Thus, for example, a clownfish could sound like a trumpet and a whale might be assigned a bassoon sound. The software also changes pitch and tempo based on the movement of the fish, thus creating a symphony of sounds based on the real-time movement of different species of fish in the tank. For someone who might be visually impaired, this technology offers a unique way to experience an aquarium. The technology can also be applied to other environments, such as zoos and museums, and instead of musical sounds, the objects can be coded as narration or other forms of output. Although CATEA is a center dedicated to discovering innovative assistive technologies for those who might be handicapped in some way, these projects can inspire all to experience sensory environments in creative new ways.

Once each year, the Georgia Tech research community shares its research output at the GVU Research Showcase (see http://www.gvu.gatech.edu/history). A member of the library's User Experience Department attended the research showcase and demonstrated a particular interest in the virtual aquarium project. One of the primary investigators for the National Science Foundation–funded project noted that the NSF requires user feedback as part of the grant request. The investigators were struggling with finding a location on campus to solicit feedback from a wide cross-section of individuals. The researchers wanted to observe how users of all abilities and backgrounds, not just those with visual impairments, interact with the aquarium project. Given the Georgia Tech library's centrally located building and the large number of students who use the space, the library was offered as a potential space for gathering user feedback about the aquarium project. It is notable that a spring 2010 LibQUAL+ survey indicated that 65 percent of all undergraduates use the library facility on a daily or weekly basis, so the library has the potential to reach a huge cross-section of undergraduate students.

The researchers indicated that they would require a mobile LCD screen and a computer to run a simulation of the aquarium. Members of the library worked with the Office of Information Technology to assess technology needs for hosting the project and determined that it would be possible to temporarily repurpose existing mobile LCD screens, thus enabling CATEA staff to survey library users about the project.

This collaboration illustrates how the librarians embraced the science and technology focus of the institute and wanted to share collaborative research on campus. The virtual aquarium is an ongoing project, requires minimal staff time, and also leverages existing resources, thereby incurring no financial commitment from the library. Furthermore, it creates a new line of communication between the library and CATEA, which opens up possibilities for additional unique collaborations. For example, students affiliated with CATEA have discussed working with the library staff to assess and improve the library's touch screen technologies and signage to make them more accessible for those with visual impairments. As with other projects discussed here, this collaboration leverages existing resources to minimize costs while positioning the library as a place where users can interact with "cool" research.

VIRTUAL POSTER SESSIONS FOR UNDERGRADUATE RESEARCH

The mobile LCD screens used for the aquarium project have been useful for a number of internal library projects as well as other library collaborations. Librarians maintain a strong relationship with the Office of Undergraduate Studies at Georgia Tech.

This office is focused on assessing and improving the undergraduate experience at the institute. Furthermore, many of the highest-achieving undergraduates are identified by the Office of Undergraduate Studies for prestigious scholarships and fellowship opportunities, such as Marshall, Fulbright, and Rhodes. Librarians support the efforts to honor special students who are also typically heavy library users. Large posters are created to list their achievements and how they use the library.

During the spring semester, the Office of Undergraduate Studies expressed an interest in finding a space and mechanism to recognize undergraduate students who work with Georgia Tech faculty on current research projects. Meeting with the director of the office, possibilities were brainstormed for engaging formats to present undergraduate research. One of the spaces that is often used for such presentations is the Library East Commons (LEC). The LEC space is a recently renovated area of the library that offers students flexible furniture, movable chairs and tables, adjustable lighting options, and technologies that facilitate collaboration. It is a heavily used space at all hours, particularly among undergraduate students. A variety of locations were considered, but it was determined that this LEC space, because of its popularity among undergraduates, would be the ideal location for an undergraduate research showcase. In brainstorming options for showcasing undergraduate research, one possibility suggested involved a series of live poster sessions. The space would be reserved at regular times, and students would discuss their research with passersby—the model used at many conferences.

Although it was agreed that the potential for personal contact between students conducting research and their peers would be a valuable outcome, the logistics of scheduling multiple "live" poster sessions could prove cumbersome with no guarantee that students in the LEC would demonstrate any interest in engaging with those presenting their work. Another, more preferable option included "virtual" poster sessions. The LCD monitors could be preloaded with undergraduate students presenting their work. The monitors could be set up such that the presentations would run continuously in the LEC space.

This arrangement was advantageous for a number of reasons. First, it would require less staff time and resources, the Office of Information Technology was able to procure additional LCD screens for this purpose at no cost to the library, and the poster sessions would run numerous times, thus more students could have an opportunity to see their peers' research work.

This virtual poster session collaboration with the Office of Undergraduate Studies demonstrates how library staff is continuously involved with project design and execution. Furthermore, this project also embraces the research focus of the institute, and little financial commitment from the library is required. Most significantly, however, is the fact that this project connects with undergraduate students in an area that aligns closely with the institute's emphasis on undergraduate research and student engagement.

TECHNOLOGY, ENGAGEMENT, AND OUTREACH IN ACADEMIC LIBRARIES: WHAT'S ON THE HORIZON?

Engaging Users with Real-Time Polling

Evidence from surveys suggests that almost all academic library users have access to cell phones and many students also use texting. Thus, finding a way to connect with students via emerging mobile phone technologies is a logical next step in user engagement. Some very simple surveys were conducted using a website called Poll Everywhere (http://polleverywhere.com). This service allows users to text in answers to questions posed to them via a PowerPoint presentation. Some examples of questions that could be posed to library users:

- "What do you think about the lighting in this space?" (answers: 1—just right; 2—too dim; 3—too harsh)
- "Should the library be open 24 hours?" (yes/no)
- "Are you in favor of more commons space if that means moving collections off-site?" (yes/no)

Anecdotal evidence suggests that multiple-choice questions work best. It is possible to have free-text comments enabled, but because the answers or results are publicly displayed in real time, librarians who choose to include an interactive poll in public spaces or in the classroom should be very aware of the possibility for rude, offensive, or nonrelevant language. The Poll Everywhere site allows the ability to moderate comments, so the poll creator can approve each comment that is submitted. This may be one method to deal with the issue of inappropriate comments.

Using a mobile LCD screen connected to a laptop to get a quick snapshot of user opinions about a very specific question is the most effective use of this type of technology. A dual advantage of this type of polling is that it is unobtrusive and immediate. Those who wish to ignore the poll can do so instead of having a staff member intrusively ask them to fill out a paper survey. Furthermore, the results can be shared internally and with users and external stakeholders very quickly.

TWITTER, SOCIAL MEDIA, AND THE ACADEMIC LIBRARY: SOME NEW APPROACHES

One approach to increase the number of followers for the Georgia Tech Twitter feed has been to aggressively identify student timelines and follow them. In doing so, the library's Twitter followers have steadily matched the number of students the library follows because the tendency on Twitter is for users to generally "follow followers." This approach has a dual advantage: First, students are able to communicate likes, dislikes, frustrations, and even reference questions via their timelines, and they will show up when the routine daily search for library-related tweets is performed. The other advantage is to get a sense of nonlibrary issues that may have some impact on student learning or student life. Because many library staff members serve on campus-wide committees, this type of information may allow library staff to contribute to a more nimble way of solving problems facing students.

ENGAGING USERS WITH AUGMENTED REALITY (AR)

A new app for GPS-enabled iPhones called Layar allows users to create layers of metadata so that when the camera on the phone is pointed in any direction, a layer of metadata about all the services, facilities, and other points of interest create an overlay on the screen. For example, if students are navigating campus for the first time, they could point their cameras at the library building and the app would overlay information about the library on the screen (e.g., hours and a website URL).

Adapting the Layar iPhone app or other similar mobile phone augmented reality (AR) apps offer numerous opportunities to reach out to library users. It may even be possible to detect elevation via some wireless networks in libraries, so a layer could be used to help guide users within the library stacks. Librarians at Kansas State University libraries are using Layar to help connect campus buildings with their special collections. Thus, when a user points his or her iPhone camera at a campus building, photographs from KSU special collections appear to show that building from earlier eras. AR presents librarians with yet another way to tie user engagement with emerging technologies to help achieve the goal of expanding awareness about library resources, spaces, and services.

CONCLUSION

Georgia Tech and the libraries' User Experience Department have been committed to exploring new ways of reaching undergraduates and engaging them with the libraries. The radio show, the accessible aquarium, the virtual posters, and the use of emerging technologies are just some of the many ways this department has been reaching out to engage students.

4

Perceived Ease of Use and Student Satisfaction and Engagement with the Library

Lesley Moyo, Director for Research & Instructional Services, University Libraries, Virginia Tech

INTRODUCTION

Academic libraries all over the world have entered a digital era in which many of their services and resources are now delivered via the web or other technology platforms that facilitate electronic access. In that setting, library users increasingly prefer to conduct library research independently without the assistance of library staff. Being able to conduct research independently in a networked information environment is now as common as doing personal banking online or taking an online class. These trends are driven in part by user expectations and technology facility, which in turn put a demand on how librarians plan and structure their services as they aspire to meet their users' expectations and provide support that enables them to conduct research effectively. Ease of use and convenience are key factors in use and nonuse of the library by patrons. In academic libraries where the effective use of the library may ultimately impact students' academic success, it is important to address any issues that may hinder students' use of the library. Liu and Luo (2011) conducted a study on factors, perceived influences, and satisfaction with using digital libraries, and they concluded that people who use digital libraries more frequently tend to have a more positive experience than those who use them less frequently. Given that user satisfaction influences use or non-use—and hence, user engagement with the library—academic librarians must consider ease of use and usability when designing services and address any barriers that may hinder effective access to and use of resources that they offer.

Librarians regularly conduct user surveys that seek to assess myriad variables and how they impact user perception and use of resources. Plosker (2002) not only emphasizes the need for pervasive assessment in libraries, but he also provides basic guidelines on what to measure and how to conduct user surveys. The primary purpose of such studies is to identify and address any shortfalls and barriers that might impede effective use of the library. Similarly, Miller (2004) offers some basics about developing appropriate instruments and methodology based on the objectives of a survey. User satisfaction is one of the most commonly assessed service parameters in academic libraries. It is understood that user satisfaction influences users' acceptance and use of the library (Cullen 2001; Heinrichs, Sharkey, and Lim 2005). Furthermore, it is also understood that user satisfaction is influenced by several factors, such as system effectiveness, user effectiveness, user effort, and user characteristics. According to Al-Maskari and Sanderson (2010), *system effectiveness* measures how well a given information retrieval system achieves its objectives. This is determined by the level of precision and recall of the system. *User effectiveness* refers to the accuracy and completeness with which users achieve certain goals. This is measured by "(a) the number of tasks successfully completed, (b) number of relevant documents obtained, and (c) the time taken by users to complete set tasks" (Al-Maskari and Sanderson 2010, 860). Furthermore, *user effort* refers to information searching behavior as users interact with the information retrieval system. This includes effort used in such actions as query formulation and modifications, click-throughs, review of retrieved items to select relevant material, and time spent—all of which influence user satisfaction. Ease of use factors into user effectiveness and user effort and may therefore ultimately influence user satisfaction.

Academic librarians have long grappled with issues of ease of use and usability of their information retrieval systems and other services and products that make up the portfolio of resources available to users. There has been limited research-based literature on the significance of these factors in influencing student satisfaction or engagement with the library. It is against this backdrop that this study sought to determine the impact of the perceived ease of use of library services on overall user satisfaction with the library. A survey of Virginia Tech students was conducted in the spring of 2007 by using the University of Washington's library survey design that was adapted for local use. The data collected during that survey was used as the basis for this study.

REVIEW OF THE LITERATURE

A number of authors have written about factors that influence user satisfaction in libraries and other similar institutions. Yo and Nev (2008) suggest that ease of use of digital libraries affects users' acceptance of the system and that effective use of the system ultimately depend on this acceptance. Although the study focuses on how personality traits may be a factor in resistance to change, it identifies a key connection between perceived ease of use and user acceptance and effective use of the digital library. In another study that highlights the importance of e-library system characteristics, Jeong (2011) found that "perceived ease of use can be singled out as a primary determinant of behavioral intention" (45) (i.e., intention to continue using the e-library system). Likewise, Yusoff et al. (2009) found that perceived ease of use is positively correlated to perceived usefulness of the e-library and concluded that if students find that the e-library is easy to use, they will be more willing to use it for information retrieval.

Shi, Holahan, and Jurkat (2004) explore a theory in an attempt to explain the satisfaction formation process in library users. They suggest that library user satisfaction is determined by the users' satisfaction with the information products that they retrieve and their satisfaction with the information system used to retrieve the information product. The study determined that satisfaction with the information product retrieved was the dominant factor in overall satisfaction with the library. This study seems to echo Yo and Nev's (2008) statement that perceived usefulness and perceived ease of use are the two primary factors that influence users' acceptance of a system. Venkatesh (2000) suggests a framework that explains how these perceptions are formed and how they change over time.

The studies cited earlier would seem to support the hypothesis of this current study that providing easy-to-use library products and services contributes to library users' overall satisfaction with the library. Therefore, academic libraries that wish to enhance student use of and engagement with the library should pay particular attention to the design and usability of their resources and services.

Other studies in the professional literature have identified additional dimensions of user satisfaction in libraries and highlighted the complexity of the interrelationship and interplay among the factors that influence it. For example, Heinrichs, Sharkey, and Lim (2005) use LibQual, a standard survey instrument approved by the Association of Research Libraries, to investigate the influence of three components of users' overall satisfaction with an academic library: firstly, the customer's satisfaction with overall quality of the service; secondly, the customer's satisfaction with the way they are treated; and thirdly, the customer's satisfaction with the library's support for their learning, research, and/or teaching needs. Cullen (2001, 665) explores the relationship between library service quality and user satisfaction by looking at, among other things, the gap between users' perceptions and expectations. She states:

It would seem that, in the complex interchange of customer expectations and perceptions across the services delivered by an organization, customer satisfaction at the micro level concerning an individual service will contribute to the dimensions of service quality ... a global or macro view of quality of service derived from all the services with which the customer has interacted.

The study concludes that the changing user expectations in the electronic library environment will impact service quality and overall user satisfaction ratings.

Many studies in the professional literature have concluded that library users prefer using electronic resources rather than traditional print resources primarily because of convenience or ease of use. For example, the literature cites some cases where resources available electronically did not provide the best quality and yet users still preferred to use the electronic resources because of easy and convenient access. These sentiments are also reflected in Lombardo and Condic's (2001) study of undergraduate periodical use in which the students rated the process of finding print articles more difficult than that of finding electronic full-text articles and hence preferred to use the electronic format. Ease of use and the convenience of remote access to full-text databases were significant factors in their choice of resources. Connaway, Dickey, and Radford (2011) also address the dimension of convenience and state: "Convenience is a situational criterion in people's choices and actions during the information-seeking process. The concept can include their choice of an information source, their satisfaction with the source and its ease of use, and their time horizon in information seeking" (180). Similarly, Vondracek (2007) found that comfort and convenience were the preeminent factors in students' choice of when to use the library, what resources to use, and whether to research from home/the dorm or the library's physical space. This is a common trait among today's college students. Their expectation to access everything online and in full text may sometimes be unrealistic and pose challenges that if not met might adversely impact their overall satisfaction and use of the library. One study that surveyed predominantly nontraditional college students who preferred to use public libraries rather than academic libraries for their college assignments found that ease of use and familiarity were among the factors that influenced their decision to use the public library rather than their academic library (Antell 2004).

By assessing whether ease of use is a significant factor in overall user satisfaction and by understanding the specific variables that influence user satisfaction, academic librarians can gain useful information for designing services that optimize access, navigation, and use of library resources. Because satisfaction with the library is one of the elements that influences use or nonuse of the library, addressing these could potentially improve student use and engagement with the library.

STUDY DESIGN AND METHODS

This study is a nonexperimental correlation study to determine the association between ease of use and overall satisfaction with the library. The study is based on data collected by using the survey method. The study population was made up of undergraduate and graduate students at Virginia Tech.

After completing the appropriate IRB protocols and approval, a study sample was randomly selected, drawing from the university's e-mail addresses. A total of 5,666 students were sampled from the target population and e-mails were sent to them; 1,178 responses were received (21% response rate), out of which 1,172 responses were complete or partially complete. Finally, 44 subjects opted out without completing the survey. Also, 116 cases were excluded due to incorrect completion of the survey instrument, leaving a total of 1,056 (19%) for analysis.

The survey instrument used for this study was based on the University of Washington User Survey tool that has been widely adopted by other academic libraries and has been tested for validity. The instrument was presented as a web-based survey form. This was considered the best way to reach the students and be able to capture data directly into a database that provides for easy manipulation and export. The instrument consisted of a total of 28 questions, each scored on a five-point Likert Scale. To determine the correlation between ease of use and overall library satisfaction, the question relating to ease of use and the question relating to overall satisfaction with the library were selected for analysis. The question relating to ease of use had 12 subordinate questions, each addressing the ease of use of a specific library service or resource. Each of these questions was also scored on a five-point Likert Scale.

Data were collected by using a web-based data collection instrument created with Survey Monkey, an online survey tool. A link to the data collection instrument was sent to the sample population via an imbedded link in an e-mail invitation to participate in the survey. The link was kept active to facilitate data collection from March 20 to May 15, 2007. Subjects completed and submitted the survey form online. Data from Survey Monkey were downloaded into an Excel spreadsheet and subsequently imported into SPSS for analysis.

Data Analysis and Presentation

The ease of use variable had 12 subordinate questions on specific library resources or services: (1) searching Addison, the library catalog, (2) finding books, (3) requesting material not owned by Virginia Tech, (4) finding references to articles, (5) finding electronic journals, (6) finding print journals, (7) finding multimedia items, (8) finding a computer to use in the library, (9) getting help, (10) using the library website, (11) getting research assistance from a librarian, and (12) managing personal library accounts. These 12 variables were converted into one composite variable by using SPSS. This composite variable for ease of use was analyzed in conjunction with the variable for overall library satisfaction to determine their relationship.

The Pearson's Correlation Coefficient statistical test was run to assess the impact of ease of use factors on overall satisfaction with the library. Pearson's Correlation Coefficient is a standardized measure of strength of relationship between two variables. It can take any value from −1 to +1. When the value is between 0 and +1, it indicates that as one variable changes, the other variable also changes in the same direction by the same amount. This is also referred to as *positive correlation*. When the value is between 0 and −1, it indicates that as one variable changes, the other one also changes in the opposite direction by the same amount. This is also referred to as *negative correlation*. A value of 0 means as one variable changes, the other does not change at all.

Before running the correlation test, a reliability test of the 12 variables used to compute the ease of use variable was tested for reliability using Cronbach's Alpha index. A reliability test ensures the ability of a measure to produce consistent results when the same entities are measured under different conditions. Cronbach's Alpha is an index of reliability that allows a researcher to measure the internal consistency of scale items based on the average inter-item correlation and indicates the extent to which the items in a given questionnaire are related to each other. The higher the Cronbach score, the more reliable the scale is. Any score of .70 or greater is generally considered to be acceptable. A score of .90 or greater indicates high reliability, while a score of .80 to .89 indicates good reliability. A score of .70 to .79 indicates acceptable reliability. A score of .65 to .69 indicates marginal reliability. There are instances when low reliability scores of <.65 can be used.

When scores are unacceptable, researchers usually review the scale and remove those variables that account for the overall low score. As seen in Table 4.1, the reliability test for these variables resulted in a high score of .924, indicating that the 12 variables that were converted into a single composite variable are appropriate for measuring ease of use. As reflected in Table 4.2 in the "Cronbach's Alpha If Item Deleted" column, there is only one variable (Find Computer in Library) that would result in improving the

Table 4.1

Cronbach's Alpha Index of 12 Variables Used to Create Ease of Use Composite Score

Reliability Statistics	
Cronbach's Alpha	**N of Items**
.924	12

Table 4.2
Cronbach's Alpha Index of Individual Variables Measuring Ease of Use

	Item-Total Statistics			
	Scale Mean If Item Deleted	Scale Variance If Item Deleted	Corrected Item-Total Correlation	Cronbach's Alpha If Item Deleted
Search Addison	23.40	66.032	.665	.919
Find Book	23.26	65.250	.692	.918
Request Non-VT Material	23.12	64.368	.689	.918
Find References to Articles	23.16	64.159	.754	.915
Find E-Journals	23.25	64.513	.737	.916
Find Print Journals	23.14	64.347	.780	.914
Find Media Items	22.95	64.380	.674	.918
Find Computer in Library	23.22	67.023	.513	.925
Get Help	23.36	66.654	.684	.918
Use Website	23.46	65.896	.711	.917
Ask Librarian for Research Assistance	23.28	65.800	.632	.920
Manage Library Account	23.35	65.312	.677	.918

current score from .924 to .925. However, given that the current score is already very high, it was decided to retain all 12 variables, as reflected in Table 4.2. When the item total statistics indicate that the removal of an item may result in a significant improvement of the Cronbach's Alpha score, it means that the score in question may not be contributing meaningfully to the composite scale and may have to be removed. In this case, it was not necessary to remove the item as the effect on the Cronbach score would be very minimal. Moreover, all the 12 variables covered questions that represented major domains of library services; therefore, it was considered important to incorporate them all in composing the ease of use variable.

A factor analysis was conducted by using the Principal Component Analysis extraction method to confirm that the 12 variables being measured did indeed relate to the construct of ease of use. Once the reliability and factor analysis were completed, the "ease of use" variable was computed from a mean composite score of the 12 subordinate variables named in Table 4.2. A Pearson's Correlation Coefficient analysis was then run to measure the impact of the "ease of use" composite variable on the 'overall satisfaction' variable.

RESULTS

As indicated earlier, the Pearson's Correlation Coefficient (r) is measured in terms of distance between -1.0 and +1.0. When Pearson's Correlation Coefficient is close to 1, it means a strong relationship between the two variables being tested. Therefore, changes in one variable are strongly correlated with changes in the second variable. Conversely, when Pearson's Correlation Coefficient is close to 0, it means a weak relationship

Table 4.3

Correlation between Ease of Use of Library Products and Services and Overall Satisfaction with the Library

		Correlations	
		Ease Of Use	**Overall Satisfaction**
Ease of Use	Pearson Correlation	1.000	.568**
	Sig. (2-tailed)		.000
	N	1043.000	1027
Overall Satisfaction	Pearson Correlation	.568**	1.000
	Sig. (2-tailed)	.000	
	N	1027	1040.000

**Correlation is significant at the 0.01 level (2-tailed).

between the two variables being tested. Therefore, changes in one variable are strongly correlated with changes in the second variable.

As reflected in Table 4.3, the Pearson's Correlation Coefficient for this test shows that r = .568, with a significance value (i.e., p value) of .000. For the correlation to be statistically significant, the p value has to be less than or equal to .05. In this test, p<0.01, indicating a statistically significant positive correlation between the two variables. The r value of .568 means that 32 percent (i.e., $.568^2 \times 100$) common variance exists between the two variables. This means that 32 percent of the variability in the "ease of use" variable can be explained by variance in the "overall satisfaction" variable. Simply put, "ease of use" constitutes 32 percent of the measure of "overall satisfaction" with the library. These results led to the conclusion that ease of use of library services and resources is a significant factor in overall satisfaction with the library, therefore supporting the study hypothesis.

SUMMARY AND CONCLUSIONS

This study sought to determine whether ease of use of library services and resources was a factor in overall satisfaction with the library among students by using the Virginia Tech University Libraries. This was important because the literature indicates that satisfaction with the library is a key factor in library usage. The study design involved the creation of a composite of all variables relating to ease of use and determining whether they were correlated to the overall library satisfaction variable. Using a Pearson's Correlation Coefficient analysis, the study determined a significant correlation between perceived ease of use and overall satisfaction with the library. These findings are congruent with findings of other studies that have explored factors that influence use and nonuse of e-libraries.

The implications of these findings, particularly in academic libraries, are that when selecting and designing services and products geared to students, ease of use or usability and convenience should be key considerations. The relationship between perceived ease of use and student satisfaction with the library has often been stated anecdotally. Statistical results of this study provide concrete data to support efforts for improving library use among students by identifying and addressing potential areas of difficulty that might impede student engagement with the library.

Limitations of the Study

The study notes that participants who respond to library surveys tend to be the ones who are more satisfied with the library than others. Therefore, the results of this study may show greater satisfaction with the library than the average satisfaction of the target population.

Suggestions for Further Research

Ease of use is just one of the many factors that influence overall user satisfaction and engagement with the library. Further studies on other dimensions of satisfaction that not only influence users' perceptions of the academic library but also their research behaviors should continue to be conducted to shed more light on areas that libraries should address in order to enhance students' library research experiences and their engagement with the library.

REFERENCES

Al-Maskari, Azzah, and Mark Sanderson. "A Review of Factors Influencing User Satisfaction in Information Retrieval." *Journal of the American Society for Information Science and Technology* 61, no. 5 (2010): 859–868. doi:10.1002/asi.21300.

Antell, Karen. "Why Do College Students Use Public Libraries? A Phenomenological Study." *Reference & User Services Quarterly* 43, no. 3 (2004): 227–236.

Connaway, Lynn Sillipigni, Timothy J. Dickey, and Marie L. Radford. "If It Is Too Inconvenient I'm Not Going After It: Convenience as a Critical Factor in Information-seeking Behaviors." *Library and Information Science Research* 33, no. 3 (2011): 179–190. doi:10.1016/j.lisr.2010.12.002.

Cullen, Rowena. "Perspectives on User Satisfaction Surveys." *Library Trends* 49, no. 4 (2001): 662–686.

Heinrichs, John H., Thomas Sharkey, and Jeen-Su Lim. "Relative Influence of the LibQual Dimensions on Satisfaction: A Subgroup Analysis." *College and Research Libraries* 66, no. 3 (2005): 248–265.

Jeong, Hanho. "An Investigation of User Perceptions and Behavioral Intentions Towards the e-Library." *Library Collections, Acquisitions, and Technical Services* 35, no. 2–3 (2011): 45–60. doi:10.1016/j.lcats.2011.03.018.

Liu, Ziming, and Lili Luo. "A Comparative Study of Digital Library Use: Factors, Perceived Influences, and Satisfaction." *The Journal of Academic Librarianship* 37, no. 3 (2011): 230–236. doi:10.1016/j.acalib.2011.02.015.

Lombardo, Shawn V., and Kristine S. Condic. "Convenience or Content: A Study of Undergraduate Periodical Use." *Reference Services Review* 29, no. 4 (2001): 327–337.

Miller, Lynette. "User Satisfaction Surveys." *Australia Public Libraries and Information Services.* 17, no. 3 (2004): 125–133.

Norris, Sonya Schryer. "Real Simple? Exploring Online User Satisfaction in Michigan." *Library Journal* 131, no. 18 (2006): 34–36.

Nov, Oded, and Chen Ye. "Users' Personality and Perceived Ease of Use of Digital Libraries: The Case for Resistance to Change." *Journal of the American Society for Information Science and Technology* 59, no. 5 (2008): 845–851.

Plosker, George R. "Conducting User Surveys: An Ongoing Information Imperative." *Online* 26, no. 5 (2002): 64–68.

Shi, Xi, Patricia J. Holahan, and M. Peter Jurkat. "Satisfaction Formation Process in Library Users: Understanding Multisource Effects." *The Journal of Academic Librarianship* 30, no. 4 (2004): 122–131.

Venkatesh, Viswanath. "Determinants of Perceived Ease of Use: Integrating Control, Intrinsic Motivation, and Emotion into the Technology Acceptance Model." *Information Systems Research* 11, no. 4 (2000): 342–365.

Vondracek, Ruth. "Comfort and Convenience? Why Students Choose Alternatives to the Library." *Portal: Libraries and the Academy* 7, no. 3 (2007): 277–293.

Yusoff, Yusliza Mohd., Zikri Muhammad, Mohd Salehuddin Mohd Zahari, Ermy Syaifuddin Pasah, and Emmaliana Robert. "Individual Differences, Perceived Ease of Use, and Perceived Usefulness in the e-Library Usage." *Computer and Information Science* 2, no. 1 (2009): 76–83.

5

Invisible Connections: Creating Community through Oral Storytelling in the UAS Listening Project

Wendy Girven, Public Services Librarian/Assistant Professor of Library Science, University of Alaska Southeast

INTRODUCTION

The Listening Project is a program that started on the campus of the University of Alaska Southeast (UAS) in April 2010 as an outgrowth of the One Campus, One Book (OCOB) initiative. A series of recording sessions of oral interviews between students, faculty, and staff on the UAS campus, the Listening Project is an effort to increase student success and engagement on campus, creating a welcoming environment on campus by reflecting the student voice. This chapter will focus on how the project was developed and undertaken by UAS librarians, including details of development and integration into the curriculum. Additionally, the influence of the project on campus culture concerning student engagement and ultimately the view of the library among students and faculty will be examined.

UAS is a small, rural campus in Juneau, Alaska, with two additional campuses in Ketchikan and Sitka, Alaska. This project was primarily held on the Juneau campus; therefore, references to UAS will be limited to that campus throughout this chapter. With a diverse student population divided between full-time, part-time, distance, and on-campus students, UAS has many unique offerings for scenery, activities, and academic opportunity but struggles with student retention and engagement. The Chancellor's Task Force for Student Success began meeting in Fall 2009 and was charged with seeking ways to engage in this unique campus environment. Students were invited to attend these meetings and share their perceptions with the committee.

Students on campus expressed a lack of connection to their peers and faculty, a desire for better programming and events that were well advertised and attended, and a need for better communication. In an effort to create these opportunities for students to interact on campus and enable a stronger sense of campus community, the committee decided to act on a proposed initiative: OCOB, a program that provides the campus with a way to share a common reading experience. The intention for the OCOB was the distribution of the book to incoming students at orientation and to be used as a theme in the classroom to create a shared experience and venue for creating community on campus. Michael Ferguson notes in his article on the use of common read programs to create community on campus:

[T]his emphasis on building community has made common reading especially appealing. Moderated discussions of the reading can bring the diversity of student viewpoints to the fore and provide an occasion for modeling the intellectual engagement with different ideas that is expected in college. (2006, 8)

The Task Force felt that the associated programming would really enhance the program and make it a more viable experience to grow community than relying solely on classroom use and discussion. With this new endeavor for student engagement proposed, planning for OCOB was led by UAS librarians. Library faculty members were primarily responsible for selecting and presenting a title to the task force. They were also charged with coordinating the associated programming for the year's activities and events. The selection for the book was *Listening Is an Act of Love* by the StoryCorps Foundation, a collection of transcribed interviews from the StoryCorps Project.[1] The project was designed as an initiative to record the lives of everyday people across the United States. This title was chosen because of the theme, accessibility for many levels of readers, and the opportunity storytelling provides to engage the student voice. Additionally, storytelling is an oral tradition of the Native Alaskan people and provides a way to highlight relevance and importance of this tradition to the UAS community. After a title was selected, a small team was assembled to manage the project, including staff from the library, the Learning Center, and Media Services.

This book selection naturally led to the idea of doing a similar storytelling and oral story recording on the UAS campus. The need for related programming and activities to support a successful OCOB initiative led to the birth of the UAS Listening Project. Librarians saw the opportunity to collaborate with Media Services in the creation of oral recordings of students, faculty, and staff. This project eventually led to more than 65 recorded stories shared by UAS campus members during the spring and fall 2010 semesters.

The librarians chose to focus the OCOB selection and related projects on the idea of storytelling for several reasons. First, they wanted students and the greater campus community to feel that they had a voice and that their story helped create the culture and environment where they live. Many students are connecting through social networking sites, such as Facebook, and participating in digital storytelling through those venues. Oral storytelling provides an opportunity to make a physical connection with their campus peers by participating face-to-face and in the classroom. Secondly, storytelling is part of the oral tradition of the Native Alaskan people on whose land the UAS campus is located. The campus strives to incorporate this cultural perspective into projects and programs that are initiated on the campus. Thirdly, the oral storytelling process is very different from essay writing or art shows, which all also showcase the student voice on campus. The project goal was to capture student stories in their own voice, allowing them to speak for themselves and preserving the current culture of UAS in spoken word.

PROJECT PLANNING/LAYOUT

The aim and scope of the project was to highlight and promote the presence of the student voice on the campus. The project would also be extended to include faculty and staff on campus and thereby increase the sense of community on the UAS campus. To create a foundation of how to conduct the sessions, librarians contacted another community in Alaska that did oral story recordings. The Petersburg Listening Project[2] in Petersburg, Alaska, was sponsored by the Petersburg Public Library. Through a grant from the Alaska State Library, the library invited the local community to be interviewed by a project facilitator and have the clip archived and shared online as well as in other local venues. Collecting information from the Petersburg experiences, librarians were able to establish a set process for how to conduct the interviews.

Procedurally, participants were encouraged to bring an interviewer to the 30-minute recording session. This could be any person of the participants' choosing, such as a classmate, friend, or family member. If the participant chose to come alone, the project provided a volunteer interviewer to help facilitate the interview process. Volunteers comprised of members from the campus community were trained by library faculty according to the Oral History Association Best Practices for Oral History guidelines.[3] These guidelines helped the project coordinators determine methods for providing information to the participants prior to the interview, respecting the rights of the interviewer during the interview process, and avoiding misrepresentations of the interviewers words when editing and publishing clips of the interviews.

The decision was made to keep a brief log of each of the interviews. These logs of keywords and ideas as the interview develops would help later in the editing process as well as provide an outline of the interview for interested persons. Because the university collected and archived the stories, a legal release form was signed by each participant. The legal release turned over rights of the recordings to the university to reproduce, broadcast, and edit the stories. Participants also filled out an optional information sheet documenting their age, birthplace, and relationship with their interviewer. Additionally, IRB paperwork was filed with the university. All the project paperwork is stored in the archive with the recordings.

From April through November 2010, the UAS Listening Project undertook a series of recordings over three weeklong sessions. The April pilot session had 20 interviews and included the work of 10 project volunteers. The pilot session helped iron out the technical aspects of the process as well as gauge community interest for participation. With the pilot filled to capacity and several waitlisted participants, the project had enough support for a full launch in the fall semester. The October and November sessions had 25 participant slots per week. Each interview was given a 30-minute time recording time, plus time for paperwork, equipment testing and setup, and questions. The scope of the project limited participation to students, staff, and faculty of UAS due to IRB guidelines.

Excerpts from selected recordings were added to the project blog,[4] and full-length MP3 and WAV recordings are held in the Egan Library for circulation and archiving. Additionally, each participant received an audio copy of his or her recording.

LAUNCHING THE PROJECT

Librarians needed to learn to use the recording equipment in order to train project volunteers, and they relied heavily on the support and collaboration of the campus Media Services. Partnering together, the two units decided on an appropriate setup of equipment, including microphones, audio mixers, and computer software.

Signups for the project were held in the student commons area of the cafeteria the week prior to the project. Students self-selected to participate in the project after learning about it in their classrooms or at the signup table. Librarians visited multiple classrooms to promote participation in the project.

To increase visibility, the recordings were taken near a busy and vibrant location on campus near the dining commons, an area frequented by students. This location provided a high profile to the project and also allowed for recruitment of more participants.

Several vital elements were needed to create a successful trial of this project. First, a similar scale project had not been attempted on campus previously, so promotion to the campus community was a primary concern. Secondly, an important aspect of launching the project campus-wide was developing opportunities for faculty support of this project. To truly be targeted for student success, the project needed the interest and support of the teaching faculty. Integration with the curriculum was noted as vital for the launch of a project of this nature and in its first attempt on campus. Many of the faculty who were part of the initial task force offered support of on-campus promotion and extra credit opportunities for students who participated in either the storytelling or the production aspect of the recordings. Library faculty, along with other faculty representatives from the task force, unveiled the project at the spring faculty convocation meeting and worked to promote awareness through faculty meetings and other avenues for campus promotion. With these efforts, a librarian was invited into multiple classrooms to advertise the project for student participation.

COLLECTING THE STORIES

Partnering with key faculty in the Communications and English departments, librarians were able to assemble a team of volunteers to support the pilot and subsequent sessions of the project. Some faculty offered credit for participation to students who were willing to help in the collection and editing processes. Librarians set up training sessions on how to use the Audacity recording software, the technical use of the equipment, and the interviewing methods. As previously stated, general guidelines of the Oral History Association were followed and used in the training process. Volunteers listened to sample stories, created sample logs, and performed mock interviews with each other. This training experience also allowed for interaction between the students, faculty, and staff who participated as volunteers, creating a sense of community among the group.

To create visibility and interest during the pilot week, the recording session was set up near the campus dining hall, a busy location central to campus. The week prior, librarians visited classrooms to share details about the project and held signups in the library and other campus locations. The pilot session had 20 recording spaces available, and all were filled quickly—by campus staff and students. This model was used for the two following sessions in fall 2010, with a change in recording location and equipment to ensure capturing the best audio possible. Recordings were made by seated participants by using two microphones, a sound mixer, a laptop, and Audacity recording software.

After each session was finished, volunteers saved the recording and made a backup file burned to CD. Small edits, such as the removal of loud noises and preinterview noise, were made to polish the file, and a copy was made available for each participant to take home. Participants had two weeks after the recording to opt out of the release and choose not to have their story archived. After that time passed, librarians made archive-quality copies for the library collection.

CREATING COMMUNITY

In order to encourage participation and help promote the project across campus, librarians shared clips of interviews from the April 2010 pilot session at new student orientation in Fall 2010.

[They] used my story for Fall orientation. I'm glad they did, a lot of students remembered it. They listened to it and remembered it and other students and I have a connection, even if I don't know their name. They feel like they know someone from a story or two. I think that builds community . . . you have that opening and opportunity to become friends. (Lumba 2010)

This was the first introduction of the UAS Listening Project blog, which houses short clips of selected stories after they are recorded. The project volunteers select a clip that presents a short story or theme from the overall interview. Each online clip is tagged with key terms so visitors to the website can select stories by theme, by type (student, faculty, or staff), and also by date. The tags provide one way that listeners can interact with the stories online by selecting themes or topics they are interested in hearing. It was hoped that the website would be enticement for participants to listen to the full interviews as well as consider sharing their own story with the community. Throughout the course of the semester, I added story clips to the project blog and promoted it through campus advertising and social media.

Each story has a storyteller, an interviewer, and a production assistant present during the recording. As stated previously, the storyteller sometimes brought an interviewer, but other times, a project volunteer sat in on the session in that role. For 30 minutes, the storyteller has center stage; he or she can recall a loved one, recount a memorable experience, and/or capture a glimpse of the storyteller in this time of his or her life. The interviewer would encourage the storytelling process by avidly listening and would ask questions as appropriate to propel the process forward. Many students who shared their stories were very open to the idea of sitting down with a stranger to tell their story instead of bringing in an interviewer.

The topics presented in the stories ran a wide range—from universal themes of family, growing up, and education as well as local culture. Many students shared stories of family members they remembered, stories of travel, and goals for the future. Multiple languages, including Native Alaskan languages—Tlingit, Haida, and Yu'pik—were recorded. The cultural background of the storytellers ranged widely, and students and staff were represented equally in the participation of the project as volunteers and as storytellers.

Of course, the crucial part of this project lies in the idea that stories are meant to be heard. The vision was to share these stories on multiple levels with our community and engage students with the stories of their campus community. The actual recording took place with an individual listener in the project booth and in the presence of a production assistant. This often created a real connection between the storyteller and listener, even if they were unknown to each other prior to the recording. The production assistants often commented on the unique role of being a silent observer of the storytelling process and what a privilege it was to participate in something so intimate and personal. After recording several sessions for other students, a production assistant remarked:

A lot of times, you don't have much interaction with other students unless you are in a class and the classroom interaction is different. Sitting down and listening to what is important to people, learning an intimate detail of someone's life.... You know something personal about them, because you know something about them; you realize how human they are. You feel an invisible connection. (Hansen 2010)

The audience setting is another venue for hearing the stories. Listening to these stories in the classroom was an additional way the stories were presented to the campus community. During the fall semester, nine faculty members invited me into the classroom for one-hour long sessions on storytelling and this project. In these sessions, students read assigned stories from the StoryCorps book (Isay 2007) and then listened to clips from the Listening Project collection. Many students noted the difference between reading personal narrative and hearing a story in the speaker's voice. Also, the students often noted that listening to a local person's story shows the importance of the individual to the makeup of the community. In an interview conducted with student participants, one remarked: "It makes the person feel important, it validates their presence. It makes you feel like you contributed something" (Hansen 2010).

Students also observed that often through media, they do not hear varied perspectives, but in storytelling, they gained different vantage points on history, community, and culture. Student discussions often pointed out the disparity between the influence of national media and celebrity over local and community culture. Hearing classmates' stories helped students look at their local community with new perspective. One senior involved in the project commented:

I recorded in April during the launch, I originally wanted to have my mom come in and tell her story, but she's pretty shy about technological stuff.... So I did the interview with Katie [UAS staff member].... I went in not knowing what I would talk about. I knew I wanted to talk about my mom; she's an influential person in my life. I talked about a lot of things, living in the Philippines, going to school there, growing up, about family. It's easy to forget these things because you are busy with life, work, and school. It was neat to sit down and reflect this is who I am, what I'm doing. (Lumba 2010)

She continued by adding how her perspective changed as she continued her involvement with the project as a volunteer:

Being able to be one of the techs to be able to listen to other people stories, I kind of enjoyed that more [than telling my own story} ... Getting to hear what other people experience, to soak it in and know something about that person, know something about them from a story they told or something they experience.

Another student commented: "It's good to listen to other people's stories and break down stereotypes. You know something about them that is personal" (Hansen 2010).

The Listening Project stories were also shared on the UAS radio show by the student Media Club—broadcast on air and via the Internet. As part of its weekly show, the Media Club broadcast stories from the project blog on air and helped to promote the project to listeners by sharing the why and how of the recording sessions. The Media Club reported receiving calls of interest regarding the project and asking for repeats of stories previously aired. One of the students involved in Media Club describes the process:

Every Sunday night we have a radio show. It's a college radio show (hosted by students). We share poetry and spoken word, campus news and events, the UAS Listening Project and music. The whole thing of the show is student voice and student involvement. With the UAS Listening Project... we were all participants with the project; we talk about the project and where it came from, and how it is a community project. We play the show on air and whoever is listening to the show is listening to the project. We've gotten feedback and people really enjoy it. I've played clips in Yu'pik for Native history month and it's really cool for students to hear it. People call and ask to have the clips played again. (Lumba 2010)

Students living in campus housing and working as Community Advisors (CAs) put together a story circle event for residents to engage fellow students in the project. They collected a series of questions to share with students to ask each other at an evening event. Additionally, the CAs used the project as a theme in their monthly bulletin boards by using the stories. The bulletin boards advertised the OCOB project and the Listening Project, advertised the story circle, and promoted participation in the overall campus program.

The project had a profound effect on the student volunteers involved as well as those participating. A Media Club student commented:

It's gotten me involved in different forms of media and storytelling, doing more with community building. It has made me want to get involved with film and photography. It helped me as a student, I'm going to pursue classes in media, do an internship with the radio. I'm nerdy about it. (Lumba 2010)

Another student felt positive about her overall experience with the project by commenting: "Getting to listen to other people's story was cool and I am more tech savvy now. I would be willing to do something like this again in the future and volunteer" (Hansen 2010).

To best illustrate the sense of community that developed from these stories, here is an example of how the storyteller and the listener interacted outside of the booth. One of the stories reflected on how a student, Ricky, had received his Tlingit name as a young adult (Tagaban 2010). He spoke of the clan he is from and how his name was given to him by an Elder and mentor. The name is illustrated by an oral story called Sandy Raven, which tells of a Totem pole that has been lost in a flooded river out to sea but is eventually brought back to the community and discovered on the beach by Raven. This clip is available on the project website.[5]

Later, when I sat down with Nicole and Grace—students who participated first as storytellers and then later as interviewers and production assistants—they mentioned the story from Ricky and how hearing it had impacted them. Grace commented: "[L]istening to Ricky's story about getting his name, he's a peer. It makes Native culture and history more available to me. Getting to hear the stories builds understanding" (Lumba 2010).

Nicole agreed by saying: "Getting to hear Ricky's name and how he got it, hearing the story behind it. Knowing that he has the responsibility to carry it on, that name. I had no idea about that, it was neat to learn." She continues by saying:

When somebody has a microphone in front of them or just like is asked these questions, it's interesting to see how willing they are to share and that creates a sense of connection between people. (Hansen 2010).

LIBRARY IMPACT

During this interview the librarian asked how the project changed their perspective of the library or library services. The students felt that they viewed the project positively but did not associate it directly with the library despite the fact that it has been coordinated and run by librarians. However, they said they felt more engaged by library staff because they had gained familiarity with them from doing this project.

One student mentioned feeling more comfortable in the library and could approach the service desks more easily because she gained a relationship with the librarians and staff through this project. "The library has always been my favorite place on campus. It [the project] makes the whole thing personable. You have connections with people and recognize them. You've shared something. It brings you closer" (Lumba 2010). The other student commented: "It makes the library more personable. When I go to the library, I see you and it makes me feel more welcome. I have no qualms about asking questions now. In that sense, it makes the library less intimidating" (Hansen 2010)."

The project also brought the library to the forefront of a major campus project, highlighting its faculty, staff, and services to other departments on campus. This project led to closer working relationships not only with the many students involved but also in the other academic and administrative units at the university.

It is particularly important to note that this project brought the library into the spotlight on the UAS campus—with individual faculty connections and overall publicity of the library facility and its faculty and services. Librarians were invited to participate in classroom sessions on the subject of the project, sharing stories from the project and talking about oral storytelling with students.

I was also invited to participate in the Alaska Anthropological Association conference as a presenter for a session on oral history. This opportunity enabled the creation of partnerships with other oral history professionals throughout the state and represented the library in a discipline-specific subject.

OUTCOMES/ FUTURE DIRECTIONS

The success of this project in its pilot and first year has made it possible for the project to continue. Current plans include having recording sessions held annually each fall, possibly partnering with a credit course to help sustain the volunteer labor required to carry it out effectively. The success of this project also led to an official OCOB committee for future selections and activities. The UAS administration has offered continued support to sustain this project into future years. A student participant said: "In the future, someone can hear your story. It's cool to think that in thirty years, your story could still be heard on campus. I like the idea of continuing for a week, once a year, letting people come in and use their voice. I think it definitely helps with student engagement" (Hansen 2010). With the library's effort to archive these stories, the opportunity exists to capture and preserve institutional memory.

The UAS Listening Project engaged students with their peers and academic staff on campus. It showed the library as a vibrant, community-driven resource for students. Additionally, the project brought library staff and faculty out of the library and integrated them more visibly on campus. This is reflected in students' perspectives through their increased comfort with staff as well as being exampled by my participation in non-library professional conferences. It also highlighted the role of the library as an archival repository, preserving these individual, local, and community stories over time. The project grew out of student requests for community-building initiatives and aimed to accomplish this by creating an avenue for the student voice on campus, which was able to be shared student to student.

NOTES

1. http://storycorps.org
2. http://listeningprojectpsg.wordpress.com
3. http://www.oralhistory.org/do-oral-history/principles-and-practices
4. http://www.uaslisteningproject.wordpress.com
5. http://uaslisteningproject.wordpress.com/2010/11/08/ricky-tagaban

REFERENCES

Ferguson, Michael. "Creating Common Ground: Common Reading and the First Year of College." *Peer Review* 8, no. 3 (2006): 8–10.

Hansen, Nicole. Interview with Wendy Girven. Digital Audio Recording. Juneau, November 20, 2010.

Isay, David. *Listening Is an Act of Love: A Celebration of American Life from the StoryCorps Project*. London: Penguin Press, 2007.

Lumba, Grace. Interview with Wendy Girven. Digital Audio Recording. Juneau, November 20, 2010.

Tagaban, Ricky. Interview with Beatrice Franklin. Digital Audio Recording. Juneau, October 19, 2010.

6

Engaging Undergraduates in Research: Exploring Students' Research Behavior and Rewarding Outstanding Use of Library Resources

Emily Daly, Coordinator of Upper Level Instruction
and Librarian for the Program in Education, Duke University

Undergraduate researchers—students engaging in graduate-level mentored research that culminates in a thesis or major project—comprise a user group more and more librarians are considering in their outreach endeavors. Efforts include recognizing outstanding research with library prizes, coordinating personal librarian programs, providing course-specific instruction to students enrolled in honors research seminars, scheduling research consultations mandated by students' departments, and designating building space specifically for undergraduates engaging in high-level research. The connection between librarians and library collections and undergraduate researchers is an obvious one, and the increasing level of importance that universities are placing on undergraduate research underscores the need for librarians to attend to the interests of these particular users.[1]

Attention to undergraduate researchers is certainly evident in the outreach initiatives at Duke University Libraries. Duke librarians designed a year-long study of nine honors researchers to learn more about how the library fit or did not fit into these undergrads' research experiences.[2] In an ongoing effort to learn more about undergraduates' research processes and their work with library materials, the Libraries also reward students for their outstanding use of library collections and services with the Robert F. Durden Prize, awarded to three or four undergraduates each year.

INTERVIEWING HONORS RESEARCHERS AT DUKE UNIVERSITY

In 2005, Duke University's administration set a goal to double the number of undergraduates who complete honors theses or projects and thereby "graduate with distinction." In May 2010, Duke achieved its goal: 26 percent of the 2010 graduating class completed honors theses or projects; in 2005, just 12 percent of the graduating class earned this distinction. The number continues to grow in every department on campus.[3] The university has developed extensive support mechanisms for these students: honors seminars, a dean and office to oversee the distinction program, and an annual symposium; Duke's librarians have worked with key stakeholders on campus to ensure they are an integral part of this infrastructure.[4] The initiative is also echoed in Duke University Libraries' strategic plan: "Sharpening Our Vision, 2010–2012," which places an emphasis on librarians' ability to engage with faculty, staff, and students at multiple points in their research.[5]

While the Libraries' specialized support services, including study carrels, a group study room, extended check-out privileges, and lockers for honors researchers, have been well received, librarians did not necessarily have a clear picture of the research process from undergraduates' viewpoints before designing services, tools, and resources for this community. In an attempt to increase the understanding of the research perspective of this user group, a user study was designed that documented and analyzed how students navigate their thesis projects from formulating research questions to writing their final products.

Before beginning the study, I met with the Directors of Undergraduate Studies (DUS) in five departments: biology, English, history, public policy, and Program II. DUS were supportive and provided permission to recruit students who intended to graduate with distinction from their departments. Nine volunteers were recruited, representing four disciplinary areas: biology (two students); history (two students); public policy (three students); and Program II, a self-designed program of study (two students). Despite repeated attempts, it was not possible to recruit students from the English department.

Each of the nine students was interviewed three times over the course of the fall 2009 and spring 2010 semesters (see Appendix A). One interview was conducted at the beginning of students' research, one midway through their thesis process, and one after their theses were completed and submitted. Interviews ranged from 15 to 40 minutes in length, notes were taken during the interviews, and they were audio-recorded for later reference. Notes were systematically reviewed from all interviews for common themes and trends.

All participants completed the study by answering all three sets of questions, and all nine submitted theses to their departments, thereby earning graduation with distinction. One student changed advisors and departments midway through the process and essentially started and completed his thesis in one semester; otherwise, students' research processes spanned at least two academic semesters. These nine students represent 2.5 percent of the 363 students who graduated with distinction in May 2010 and .6 percent of their graduating class, which totaled 1,396 students. Five of the nine graduated with "high distinction" (one student) or "highest distinction" (four students), an honor conferred by individual departments on the basis of students' theses. Of the four departments, biology graduated the most students with distinction (59 students, or 37% of all biology majors), while Program II graduated the fewest (seven students but the highest percentage at an impressive 70 percent of Program II majors graduating with distinction). Twenty percent (22 students) of history majors and approximately 16 percent (21 students) of public policy students graduated with distinction.

All nine study participants expressed appreciation for library services tailored for honors researchers. One student said, "I thought the library would just keeping doing what the library does [when I started my thesis], but you've gone above and beyond."

All students were aware of at least some of the specialized services offered by the library (e.g., study carrels, lockers, group study room), but they took advantage of them to varying degrees.

Two students said the library needs more lockers, and other students noted that they tried to use the group study room designated for honors researchers but found it to be very crowded. Three students said they wished they had used such services as the lockers or study carrels but forgot they were available or simply never "got around to using them."

Students used a variety of methods for organizing their research, including Excel; a physical binder, notebook, or file system; sticky notes to tag portions of books and notes; an electronic file system with Word documents and electronic folders or EndNote; and an online file system, such as Papers, Zotero, or RefWorks. Three students used citation software to format their citations (two used EndNote; one began using RefWorks and then switched to Zotero). Other students either started to use a tool and then abandoned it due to its complexity or decided from the start to format citations manually.

When asked what role the Libraries played in their research and at what point the Libraries were most critical to their work, six stated that it was most crucial for locating print and electronic resources locally and through Interlibrary Loan (ILL). Four students representing three departments relied most heavily on the library as a physical space. Four students did the bulk of their work in their apartments or dorm rooms, and one student used the library and other spaces to complete her thesis. Overall, nine of the 19 human and physical resources interviewees deemed "critical" to the success of their research were related to the Libraries; students mentioned subject librarians, data services staff, ILL, and the Libraries' chat/IM service, among others.

With that said, four students indicated that the Libraries could do a better job of marketing their services and clarifying the role of the subject librarian in supporting their work. Study participants believe that students, including themselves, are generally not familiar with the research consultation service.

Just two study participants met individually with a subject librarian to discuss their research, and one e-mailed a subject librarian for search strategies and resource recommendations. It is worth noting that all three of these students received course-integrated library instruction in conjunction with the honors seminar required by their departments, and all three graduated with "highest distinction," which is the highest honor conferred by the university for students' research. Another student remarked that she "could have taken advantage of librarians' services but just didn't." She said she "would have enjoyed e-mailing back and forth with a librarian" in her field but was unclear of the role of her subject librarian in this process (note that she was also part of an honors seminar that included library instruction). One participant indicated that students "may need a push" to schedule a research consultation, suggesting that requiring honors researchers to meet with a librarian was worth exploring. She believes that "no student would have a problem with it; they just don't know it exists."

Study participants said it makes most sense to incorporate research instruction and information about specialized services the Libraries provide into honors seminars, which are offered by some departments but not all. One student believes that office hours designated for honors researchers would also be helpful; she believes other students would like to have the option of meeting with a subject specialist or data services librarian during these hours.

Two students—both in Program II—believed they did not need the Libraries for their research given the nature of their projects. One student wrote a novella based in the present-day United States, while the other developed a philosophical theory and thus had "very few citations because much of it was original." Another student, one who graduated with "highest distinction" in history, said he appreciates everything the library does but did not feel that librarians could have "added anything to his research" because it is just so "incredibly specific"; instead, he "asked his advisor or did the search [him]self." However, this same student did indicate that the Libraries were critical as he acquired primary and secondary sources from Duke and other institutions.

Over the course of interviewing these nine students, many were found to be unaware of the full extent of library services and resources available to them. For example, one student did not know that he could access library resources from off campus and rarely used the Libraries home page to access subscription resources. Two others were not aware they could request materials from other institutions until the librarian's meeting. Note that one of these students was part of an honors seminar that incorporated a library instruction session, and the other graduated not only with distinction but "high distinction." Many incorrectly named library resources and services, referring to the library catalog as the "library website" or "library search engine" or referring to a subject database as "EBSCO," but they were able to use them to meet their needs.

Overall, these nine honors researchers were confident in their abilities to complete high-level research. None mentioned "using the library" or "conducting research" in their first interviews when asked "What do you think will be the most difficult part of the whole process for you?" In their last interviews, none mentioned "using the library" or "conducting research" when asked "What was the most difficult aspect of your project?" All successfully completed theses and graduated with distinction. Three of the nine students said they would change nothing about their research process if they were to initiate another project. Those who would make changes to their research process said they would start their research earlier; focus/narrow their topic or research questions earlier; choose a different topic (one student realized midway through the process that she would be happier writing on a different subject but continued and was pleased with her final product); start the writing phase of their projects earlier while still conducting research; start using citation management software earlier or choose a different citation management tool; and "have a better plan [for citing sources] from the beginning."

Regardless of whether they acknowledged needing to change their research process, several students demonstrated gaps in their understanding of library services and the most efficient ways to access and evaluate library resources over the course of their interviews. This finding confirmed librarians' suspicions that they needed to increase support for upper-level courses so honors researchers are better prepared to conduct thesis research. These interviews also underscored the need to continue marketing citation management tools and other services the Libraries provide for honors researchers.

The benefits of this type of study are innumerable. Meeting with students three times over the course of the academic year enabled researchers to get to know them and see their research styles, questions, and processes emerge, evolve, and mature. For example, one student changed his research topic and advisor after the second interview and still managed to complete a thesis—one he is quite pleased with and plans to continue work on before the April deadline.

Another student had not begun to engage with library resources for his thesis during our first two interviews but declared in our last conversation that the experience of "writing a full science paper by myself gives me confidence that I can be a fully functioning member of a research lab—I can write and do research for science papers; I can chase sources." Others echoed this student's sentiment, saying that they "have a better grasp of [their] discipline in ways that are intangible to explain but that are fundamental and critical" and observing that their experience gave them the confidence they needed to complete high-level, independent research and that they are now "a lot less intimidated by a project like this."

Furthermore, I was able to introduce library services and resources at students' points of need while being careful to remain as objective as possible while they were answering interview questions. Their research questions were answered at the conclusion of each interview. The casual, one-on-one interview setting was optimal for students to provide positive and negative feedback about the Libraries. It was also extremely worthwhile to interview students in a variety of disciplines, working on projects ranging from scientific discovery to a piece of fiction. Students also expressed that they benefitted from the opportunity to reflect on their research processes, and they appeared to appreciate the interest taken in their research habits and needs.

Finally, this study helped librarians connect with university administration and directors of undergraduate studies. Prerecruitment meetings with DUS in biology, English, history, Program II, and public policy afforded the opportunity to highlight services the Libraries were already providing for honors researchers, and many were eager to communicate this information with their students through e-mail and departmental webpages. After discussing the completed study with colleagues in the Libraries, a report of key findings was shared with the academic deans who oversee Duke's Graduation with Distinction program. The deans, in turn, shared and discussed the report with all DUS. These university administrators gave positive feedback; like their students, they appeared to appreciate the time librarians had invested in order to develop a more informed understanding of seniors' unique perspective on the research process.

REWARDING STUDENTS' OUTSTANDING INFORMATION-SEEKING BEHAVIORS

Not only are Duke librarians interested in learning more about students' honors research experiences, but they are also committed to exploring undergraduates' engagement with library resources and services in conjunction with students' finished or nearly finished products, ranging from annotated photo essays to semester-long research papers written during mandatory first-year writing courses. A number of schools have formalized this interest in students' information-seeking behaviors into an awards program of some sort: librarians at Penn State and the University of Wisconsin–Madison confer information literacy awards and research prizes in conjunction with Penn State's Undergraduate Exhibition[6] and UW–Madison's Undergraduate Symposium,[7] university-sponsored events showcasing undergraduates' posters and presentations in a variety of disciplines. Librarians at other universities, including the University of California–Berkeley[8] and the University of Oregon,[9] reward students for outstanding research for a course paper or project independent of university poster sessions or symposia.

In 2008, Duke University librarians developed the first Robert F. Durden Prize, modeled after Berkeley's Library Prize for Undergraduate Research and named for professor emeritus of history Bob Durden. Like Berkeley's prize, applicants for the annual Durden Prize are required to submit not only research papers completed for courses taken during the previous academic year and statements of support from the faculty members who oversaw their research but also essays of approximately 500–750 words in which they describe how they planned and crafted their papers or projects.[10] Students are asked to consider a number of questions, ranging from foundational questions such as "How did you think about and refine your research topic?" to those that prompt reflection, including "What did you learn about your own research process and style?" and "What expertise have you gained as a researcher?" (See Appendix B.)

While the Durden Prize selection committee of three librarians and two faculty members certainly considers the quality of students' research papers or projects, students' finished work is secondary to their research process essays. In fact, round one of the judging process, which is conducted by librarians, focuses solely on students' research process essays, bibliographies, and the statements of support they receive from faculty members. Once librarians narrow the pool of applicants to approximately 10 finalists, the two faculty members on the selection committee join them to judge students' full application packets on the following criteria:

- Sophistication, originality, and depth or breadth in students' use of library collections (databases, primary sources, and multimedia materials)
- Students' use of library services, including research consultations with appropriate subject librarians, librarians' office hours, reference librarians' face-to-face or virtual assistance (IM/text/e-mail), and Document Delivery
- Students' ability to locate, select, evaluate, and synthesize library resources and then use them in the creation of a project that shows originality and/or has the potential to lead to original research in the future

In addition, selection committee members are interested in seeing that students have achieved significant personal learning and developed a habit of research and inquiry that will contribute to information literacy skills and serve them well in the future. Because librarians wish to reward the achievements of students at multiple points in their Duke careers, the Durden Prize is awarded to undergraduates in three categories: first- and second-year students; third- and fourth-year students; and honors thesis writers.

Librarians in particular have learned a great deal from reading applicants' research essays over the last four years. From these short essays, librarians see firsthand how students describe library resources and the Libraries' web interfaces. Even these students, whose papers and projects reflect some of the highest quality undergraduate research at Duke, frequently refer to the library catalog or even the entire library home page as the "library search engine" and demonstrate a rather limited understanding of the vast number of subject databases and discipline-specific resources the library licenses or purchases for their use. It is evident from these essays that some students leave a huge number of resources untapped simply because they believe they are unearthing everything by searching the Libraries' search engine, which they may mean to be the catalog.

Conversely, students who have a much clearer understanding of the way library resources are organized and who maximize the potential of library resources and services report: "Since this topic was very interdisciplinary, I needed to be acquainted with anthropological, religious, and linguistic databases. The major databases I utilized were ATLA, Linguistics and Language, ProQuest, Google Scholar, and JSTOR." And from another: "I started by studying the bibliography of scholarly monographs assigned for class, which allowed me to follow the train of experts on [my subject] and led me to anthologies in the Duke Library catalog." Others commented on the research style they developed as they worked on their papers: "I learned that I like to look at a range of sources, as opposed to confining my research to one medium. I ran online searches, took advantage of interlibrary loan, spent time in the Rare Book Room, and worked closely with microfilm."

Other students commented on mastering a specific aspect of information literacy, including evaluating sources:

Through this research process, I have gained a better understanding of what research really entails. I initially expected to spend the majority of my time finding resources.... Synthesizing the pieces of information so they gave me a better understanding of the events and interactions that took place was by far the most challenging and exciting part of the process.

Another applicant reported: "From a research standpoint, this ability to be selective with my sources has been the largest takeaway from my project. In our Internet age ... the skill lies in separating the scholarly and the balanced from the chaff—and incorporating one's sources in a logical manner."

A number of students noted in their essays that they grew as researchers as a result of their work:

Before my most recent undertaking, I had let my research process become a mechanized fable of convenience: For a given topic, a few books and a scholarly article or two would suffice. [This project] forced me to abandon this formulaic process and adopt a more sophisticated strategy.

Another student reported: "In addition to learning about my topic, I have acquired advanced research skills, proficiency with new software, and a better understanding of the research process." Still another noted that the work she did helped "reveal the timidity of [her] initial research approach and prepared [her] for a new boldness for the remainder of [her] project." She asserts: "I realized that stating my conclusions confidently and supporting them with evidence was also important." Another student commented on the impact the research skills he gathered will have on his career: "I hope someday to go into public policy work with an economic focus, and this project, with the help of Duke Libraries, undoubtedly helped me hone my research instincts and analytical skills."

When asked in an interview following the 2009 Durden Prize reception what insights he gained from his research, prize winner Andrew Simon said that he learned to "look at a wide range of sources rather than just going on the library's website and typing in a few keywords—really to push [myself] to try to find primary documents." He also noted that the process helped him appreciate the "amount of time you have to invest in research.... It's an intensive process, but in the end, I think the payoff is very great."[11]

Students are not the only ones who see in themselves their development as young scholars: Librarians are also encouraged by the incredible growth they see in students over the course of their careers at Duke. Individual students apply more than once—sometimes even exploring the same topic or research question from one year to the next—and the progress they make in their understanding of the nature of research and the role they play in the production of new knowledge is evident in all cases and inspiring in some. It is also gratifying to see the differences in sophistication among students based on their class at Duke. First-year students typically produce very different types of papers than do juniors or honors thesis writers, who have honed their personal writing style and tend to take advantage of a larger and more diverse array of library resources and services.

Also of note are faculty members' statements of support for students' submissions, which describe students' persistence and ability to uncover and use materials: "[This student] was extremely thorough and creative in use of all available sources, tracking down relevant materials in a wide range of locations on and off campus. I had been unaware of some of the resources she discovered" and "[This student] showed excellent critical judgment in the way she used her wide range of materials." From another applicant: "[This student's] use of the resources in Perkins Library is as thorough as it is not only because she is a diligent scholar but also because of excellent planning." Others speak to their students' sophistication and capability to contribute new insights to their field: "This is a topic of considerable economic interest; needless to say, it is *not* the sort of work usually attempted by an undergraduate." From another faculty member: "I honestly think that [this student] has the ability and determination to potentially write the first publishable biography of [the subject of this paper]. It's this paper that has convinced me that she has the research skills, the imagination, and the literary skills to pull this off."

While the most heavily represented department in Durden Prize submissions is history—perhaps because the prize is named for a professor emeritus of history—papers are received from a range of disciplines representing the social sciences, humanities, natural sciences, and physical sciences: art history, biomedical engineering, cultural anthropology, dance, economics, English, evolutionary anthropology, public policy, religion, Spanish, and women's studies, among others. Past winners have ranged in scope from a paper written for an interdisciplinary physics course on architectural acoustics and music to a thesis written for the Asian and Middle Eastern Studies department on Egyptian Christian and Muslim relations making extensive use of primary sources from Duke's Rare Books, Manuscripts, and Special Collections Library. Also represented are papers on opium suppression in late Imperial China and a thesis for the economics department that utilized the Libraries' Data and GIS Services in order to propose a propensity score matching approach for studying capital control and exchange rate policy.

While a respectable number of Durden Prize submissions have been sent in each year since 2008 (anywhere from 27 to 41 submissions in a given year, which is comparable to the number of applications for other libraries' research prizes, according to the librarians who oversee their programs), work continues to increase the number of applicants, including a number of marketing venues and methods: Facebook and Twitter posts, table tents in student centers and campus coffee shops, ads in campus buses, e-mails to students who have requested research consultations with subject librarians, and announcements in library instruction sessions and Blackboard course sites.

Two years ago, applicants were asked how they learned about the Durden Prize in an attempt to focus our marketing efforts. Their number one response was students' faculty advisors or course instructors. This finding confirms what our honors researchers told us in their interviews last year. Students tend to look first to faculty mentors for advice about and affirmation of their research, and this drives two key Durden Prize marketing strategies: e-mailing end-of-semester reminders about the prize to faculty who have requested library instruction and sending publicity postcards to every faculty member who teaches undergraduate students. We also rely on subject librarians to market the prize to faculty in their disciplines through e-mail and at department meetings.

Regardless of how many applications we receive and how students learn about the Durden Prize, the program continues to be well received by faculty members, students, and librarians alike. It is a pleasure to read the work of some of Duke University's brightest emerging scholars, and it is a joy to be able to reward them for their efforts with recognition and a cash prize. (Because the prize is currently funded by two Duke alumni, we are able to present a total of $3,000 to three or four undergraduates each year.)

Additionally, the prize and the research essay component in particular encourage these budding researchers to think critically about and reflect on their research and the role the Libraries play in their research. Furthermore, our targeted publicity of the award each semester prompts faculty members to consider the part the Libraries play in their curricula and course assignments and their students' end products.

Librarians at Duke University have employed a number of successful methods for engaging students in meaningful conversations about their research strategies and resulting projects. What has been learned? It is impossible to guess how these students conduct research or, moreover, design services for them without first asking them to consider and describe the role the Libraries play in their scholarship. Researchers' habits are as individualized and unique as the questions that drive their theses. While some conclusions about best practices for supporting undergraduates may be drawn, it is not possible to see clear lines based only on their disciplines, genders, or ages. Science students do not go to the library to work; they do all their work in the lab. This generation of students does not use note cards or paper and pen for taking notes or drafting their papers; they do everything online.

This is precisely what makes the work so interesting, but it also happens to make jobs as librarians particularly challenging. Students are encouraged to make use of library resources through work at public service desks and in research consultations and instruction sessions, and a suite of services is offered in hopes of attending to the information literacy skills and research needs of as many students as possible. Oftentimes, however, the most effective way to get to know users and their unique perspectives on the research process and to determine how they are using the library—and, perhaps more importantly, how they are maturing as scholars—is simply to ask.

NOTES

1. Stamatoplos, Anthony. "The Role of Academic Libraries in Mentored Undergraduate Research: A Model of Engagement in the Academic Community." *College & Research Libraries* 70, no. 3 (2009): 235–249.

2. Daly, Emily. "Is the Library Part of the Picture? Asking Honors Undergrads to Describe their Research Processes." *College & Research Libraries News* 72, no. 7 (2011): 408–411, 419.

3. Trinity College of Arts & Sciences, Duke University. "Graduation with Distinction." Accessed July 1, 2011. http://trinity.duke.edu/academic-requirements?p=graduation-with-distinction.

4. Duke University Libraries. "Check Out What the Library Offers Students Writing Honors Theses." Accessed July 1, 2011. http://library.duke.edu/research/undergraduate/index.html.

5. Duke University Libraries. "Sharpening Our Vision: Duke University Libraries' Strategic Plan for 2010-2012." Accessed July 1, 2011. http://library.duke.edu/about/planning/2010-2012.

6. Penn State University Libraries. "University Libraries Award for Information Literacy." Accessed May 24, 2012. http://www.libraries.psu.edu/psul/lls/infolit_award.html.

7. University of Wisconsin–Madison Libraries. "Undergraduate Research Awards." Accessed July 1, 2011. http://www.college.library.wisc.edu/resources/researchaward.

8. University of California–Berkeley Library. "Library Prize for Undergraduate Research." Accessed July 1, 2011. http://www.lib.berkeley.edu/researchprize.

9. University of Oregon Libraries. "Library Undergraduate Research Awards." Accessed July 1, 2011. http://libweb.uoregon.edu/general/libaward.html.

10. Duke University Libraries. "Robert F. Durden Prize." Accessed July 1, 2011. http://library.duke.edu/research/awards/durden/index.html.

11. Duke University Libraries. "Conversations about the Durden Prize for Undergraduate Research." Accessed July 1, 2011. http://www.youtube.com/watch?v=fMhw4Z_zEOQ.

APPENDIX A: INTERVIEW PROTOCOL FOR HONORS RESEARCHERS

Interview #1 Questions

1. What was your primary motivation in deciding to write an honors thesis?
2. How did you select your topic?
3. How did you select your faculty advisor?
4. At this point, what is your research plan?
5. What are the biggest unknowns for you at this point?
6. What do you think will be the most difficult part of the whole process for you?
7. How might the university/department/library support you as you begin to write your thesis? What are your expectations from each of these groups?

Interview #2 Questions

1. How much progress have you made?
2. Has your topic changed? How and why?
3. What role is your advisor playing at this point?
4. What resources are you using (human or physical)? Are you finding everything you need?
5. Are you finding all the research information you need? What tools are you using to find research information?
6. What tools are you using to track and organize your research?
7. Have you started writing? If so, how did you begin?
8. Do you think your research project is "on track"? If not, why not?
9. Knowing what you know now, is there anything you would have changed about your initial research plan?

Interview #3 Questions

1. Knowing what you know now, is there anything you would have changed about your research process?
2. What resources or tools were the most significant to you during your research?

3. What role did the library play in your research? At what stage of your research were library services/resources most important to you?
4. Do you think the strategy you used to organize your research was effective? Why or why not?
5. What was the most difficult aspect of your project?
6. Did you receive adequate support from your advisor? What other forms of support and guidance did you take advantage of?
7. If you had to select one or two human or physical resources that were critical to your research, what would they be? How did you find them?
8. Were there resources, services, or tools that you wish had been available to you?
9. Are you pleased with the final product?
10. Would you do this again? What did you gain from the experience?
11. Any downsides to writing a thesis? Regrets?
12. Do you plan to publish or do further work on your thesis? Is your work on DukeSpace yet?

APPENDIX B: QUESTIONS DURDEN PRIZE APPLICANTS CONSIDER WHEN WRITING THEIR RESEARCH ESSAYS

1. How did you think about and refine your research topic?
2. What specific strategies did you develop for finding relevant information?
3. What specific library search tools did you use and why?
4. What specific library services (e.g., research consultations, librarians' office hours, Document Delivery) did you take advantage of and how did these services support your research?
5. Did you have trouble finding some types or formats of information;? If so, how did you overcome this challenge?
6. Did your assumptions about what information would be available change throughout the research process?
7. Did you have some reasons for not selecting specific resources, even though they appeared promising?
8. What did you learn about finding information on your topic or in your discipline? Was it necessary to move outside your discipline to find sufficient sources?
9. How much did the sources you used provide support for your thesis or conclusions?
10. How did you balance the evidence that you found?
11. What did you learn about your own research process and style?
12. What expertise have you gained as a researcher?
13. What do you still need to learn?
14. What would you change about your strategies and process if given another chance to conduct this research?

7

Undergraduates of Opportunity: Capitalizing on Talent and Crafting Undergraduate Projects with Rare Books and Manuscripts

Sandra Stelts, Curator of Rare Books and Manuscripts,
Penn State University Libraries

Undergraduate internship programs and independent studies offered by the Special Collections Library at the Pennsylvania State University Libraries, have provided opportunities for talented students to contribute to library initiatives. They have processed important archival and manuscript collections, curated imaginative exhibitions, conducted sophisticated preservation surveys, and created innovative digital projects with their dazzling skills in photography and computer technology. This chapter will explore several projects that have provided young students with practical experience in appreciating the value of primary source materials in teaching and scholarship. The Special Collections Library has likewise benefitted from fresh approaches to learning and "marketing" collections in new ways.

Internship programs give undergraduates the opportunity to participate in active and collaborative learning and to gain work experience while earning academic credit. One program, created from an endowment established in 2000 by Donald Hamer and Marie Bednar, a former university libraries cataloger and department head, has enabled the Special Collections Library to host several interns. These paid internships are competitive, and a committee annually reviews proposals from many library departments to hire six to eight interns per year. Rare Books and Manuscripts has been fortunate to have six Bednar interns over the years, and the experience has been so satisfying and rewarding that I recently established an undergraduate internship—the Stelts-Filippelli Undergraduate Internship—so this unit might always be prepared to offer such an experience to a deserving student. Other special projects may involve unpaid undergraduate interns or independent study projects for credit—often at the request of students who wish to gain practical experience before applying to library schools.

The competence and potential of these undergraduates as they tackled projects has been pleasing and surprising to see. Sometimes, the projects seemed at first to be perhaps too advanced to entrust to young workers. All of them performed admirably, and some handled every task thrown their way with eagerness and a degree of sophistication that was not expected.

When selecting interns to pair with suitable projects, decisions were based on students' individual interests and strengths. Some interns processed manuscript and archival collections so they could claim "ownership" of online finding aids; some wrote core-level records; others prepared and installed exhibitions and gave gallery tours; one conducted a preservation survey of a 500-volume collection of emblem books; another participated in a scanning project. All of them answered reference questions, assisted with public service, performed basic preservation work, and happily entered into the daily life of the department, where priorities and duties can change instantly with the arrival of a new collection or a visiting researcher.

One intern graduated and became a writer/reporter. Two were inspired because of their processing projects to enter the publishing profession. Others went on to graduate school, including library school and a position as an academic librarian.

While there are these formal undergraduate internship opportunities at the Penn State Libraries, some recent and fortuitous experiences that grew out of classroom encounters are worth mentioning to those who are considering taking advantage of the knowledge and creativity of exceptional students.

Ted Schwab was a medieval studies major at Penn State who first contacted Special Collections in his junior year about getting experience in working with medieval materials. He was interested in pursuing an internship—either formal or informal—but he had missed the deadline for application to one of the paid undergraduate internships. Creating individual unpaid internships is somewhat tricky because of the requirements of our office of human resources for granting computer access and establishing volunteer agreements. Ultimately, Ted's work began as an independent study project with Professor Jeanne Krochalis, a medievalist at Penn State's New Kensington campus and the person who is most knowledgeable about medieval manuscripts in general and our collection in particular. She was absolutely delighted to be working with an outstanding student, and it was gratifying to witness their mutual excitement as they worked together with original manuscript leaves.

Ted's work was of great benefit in the process of digitizing and cataloging medieval materials. Ted transcribed four leaves (recto and verso) of a humanist miscellany that contained Classical and Christian authors. He identified all the authors and most of the texts and described the various hands. His work had a practical and useful purpose in that it was used as the basis for creating MARC catalog records. He was given online credit. Reference questions for long-distance researchers were often referred to Ted, and he did an admirable job.

Another enjoyable project suggested by Ted on his own initiative became a public event. He was the president of the Penn State Medieval Society, and he single-handedly engaged and enlarged the membership to make use of library resources and to promote the medieval holdings to a larger audience. He organized, publicized, and carried out with great professionalism an evening program in Special Collections that involved mounting a temporary exhibition in our classroom of a selection of medieval materials—original manuscripts and manuscript facsimiles. He rallied his club members to come for preliminary meetings to make selections. He supervised the writing and editing of explanatory labels and wrote most of them himself and put out a display that was appealing and educational. During the event, he spoke to attendees very knowledgably about the items on view. So many favorable comments were received from those who attended that Ted presented a similar program a second time.

Ted was then hooked on working with original manuscripts and subsequently entered into an official internship in Special Collections as part of an archives management course. He then enrolled in a master of arts program in public history at Duquesne University. His is a success story of the merits of engaging undergraduates and of the mutual benefits of library staff, academic faculty, and students working together to pursue mutually beneficial projects using Special Collections materials.

In 2009, Cody Goddard, a senior Schreyer Honors Scholar majoring in photography and integrative arts at Penn State, attended two classes I conducted in Special Collections: one in Professor Nancy Locke's art history class on the history of photography and the other in Professor Steven Rubin's photography class on narrative photography. Cody came to ask about the possibility of working on a "documentary" project for Professor Rubin's class, and we settled on his assisting with an exhibition in the Henisch Photo-History Collection Exhibition Room in the spring of 2009. The Henisch Collection is a vernacular collection, which means not a collection of photographs by well-known photographers but a broad assemblage of everyday photographs taken by unknown photographers that offer a rich source for nineteenth-century social history.

After the meeting, Cody wrote:

I have been thinking about how the topic relates back to photography at Penn State, as well as some of the more unusual examples of technical work in the collection. What would you think about potentially angling the show towards technical innovations and reinventions of process? That way we could talk both about what makes particular pieces in the Henisch Collection so unique, as well as ways in which current Penn State students are putting new twists on these historical processes.

We decided to display a number of older photographic processes (daguerreotypes, ambrotypes, tintypes, etc.) from the Henisch Collection, along with some of Cody's recent photographic work, which employs these same processes but from digitally printed negatives. The "angle" to be promoted was that the historic processes can be inspirational and that they can be combined with alternative processes and different techniques to create something entirely new. He agreed to write the label text and to make a selection of images.

In preparation for the exhibition, Cody spent weeks looking over the holdings of the Henisch Photo-History Collection for suitable items to display. He made detailed notes on hundreds of images, noting in particular any unusual technical features or flaws that gave away the photographers' techniques and failures. Cody's selections were unique in that one would never have normally made those particular selections for an exhibition, as damaged items would be dismissed in favor of "museum worthy" images. Cody's choices were all the more fascinating for their imperfections. The completeness of Cody's work prompted the idea that his work should not be limited to background for the exhibition alone; his expertise could be the basis of an extensive finding aid for parts of the Henisch Collection. Cody is probably still surprised that because of a class project, he ended up being the curator of an exhibition and the speaker at a public gallery talk.

Cody later photographed all 250 of the cased photographs in the Henisch Collection and worked on an independent study with Professor Locke, which will result in an unexpected digital project for the Henisch Photo-History Collection. His work passed muster with the digital projects committee which vetted the proposal and allowed the bypass of the usual procedures to produce a digital project in house.

Cody later wrote about his experiences:

My collaboration with the Special Collections library at Penn State began with an assignment for a photographic narratives course: go out onto campus and find something interesting that's happening, then document it. Having worked for the student newspaper for a couple of years, I knew what the usual suspects were and that I wanted to avoid them. I headed to the library, remembering that I had been told that Penn State had a rather large collection of daguerreotypes. For whatever reason, I had never actually gone over to see what was there. I found the exhibit in the Henisch Exhibition Room and contacted Sandra Stelts about doing a documentary photography project about the Special Collections Library and what all went on there. After we met and talked, Sandy offered me an opportunity to curate a show from the Henisch Collection's holdings. I hadn't even imagined that this would be a possibility.

There aren't many people in the world today who practice historical processes. The last count that I have read was that there are approximately 60 active daguerreotypists in the world today. More modern processes such as wet-plate collodion are currently seeing a resurgence (modern being a relative term—1850s era), but there are still not many people with in-depth knowledge of the complete process, from imaging making to final presentation. While a lot of information about "how things used to be done" can be gleaned from talking with experts in the field, some things can only be learned by holding the actual photograph-objects that were made over 150 years ago.

Over the course of the next several months I had the opportunity to hold and examine over 300 daguerreotypes, tintypes, and ambrotypes, many of which were cased. Having seen a number of fine examples of early photography, it was very illuminating to see "everyday" photographs—photographs made by average photographers for average clients.

Because I don't have a background in cultural history, I decided to base the show I would co-curate on technical aspects of photography—the particular characteristics, mistakes, and idiosyncracies of the different processes utilized. This would highlight the important differences in process and in final image quality that are inherent when using orthochromatic processes. So often when we look at old photographs we look at them as just that—old photographs. We often note how stern, haggard, and worn people look in older pictures, and we see that as a reflection of how hard life was "back then." Because daguerreotypes and wet collodion processes are sensitive only to blue light, any imperfections (blemishes, wrinkles, creases) generally show up much more prominently than how we see them. They are also much more dramatic than a modern black and white photograph. I decided to include some modern tintype portraits that I have made to show this fact—that people 150 years ago probably looked an awful lot like we do today!

Looking through such a large number of photographs actually helped me begin to understand a bit about the cultural history of that era as well—I have since learned a lot about the invention of photography and the rise in scientific inquiry that made it possible. Photography has had a dramatic impact on the development of popular culture, and in other art forms for the last hundred and fifty years. Looking at early photographs is a great way to see the earliest moments of its impact.

I don't think enough can be said for the opportunity to hold historical photographs and to examine them. Having seen over 300 cased images, I have a much broader bank of knowledge to draw from when evaluating my own work, and when looking at other historical photographs. I have seen common and uncommon approaches to solving the limitations of a photographic process 1/300 the sensitivity of our slowest modern digital cameras. Through our collaboration,

I was able to provide the Special Collections Library with a new and practical insight into the images that they had, largely because I had worked with all of the processes that I was looking at. I could explain the reasons for different visual effects, choices, and point out mistakes that had been made by the photographers. I gained valuable insight into the broader world of historic photographs.

A Bednar internship position was filled with another talented student, Brian Maynard, an undergraduate in Penn State's Schreyer Honors College majoring in interdisciplinary digital studio bachelor of design. Brian became involved with Special Collections because of a chance remark—"Can't we find some students who know how to do this?"—at a library meeting that led to a new search for help. Brian was "discovered" in an academic department at Penn State called Interdisciplinary Design Studio (IDS) in the College of Arts and Architecture, led by professors Matt Kenyon and Carlos Rosas. When an exploratory e-mail message was sent to them, an immediate and wildly enthusiastic offer of help was returned with the agreement to participate in a libraries digital project called "Transformations: Movement in Toys That Teach."

The IDS faculty and students—undergraduate and graduate—were involved in a proof-of-concept project to digitize "movable objects" (beginning with early nineteenth-century "flap books") from Special Collections and to highlight them as the initial building blocks for a scholarly, interdisciplinary website built around the theme of "transformation" in a broad sense in cultural history and in the use of current technology. It was following the general theme of "toys that teach," including books, maps, craft projects, games, and building blocks, among others.

We were already into the discovery phase to investigate, test, and demonstrate what can be done with technology as well as to highlight some of the most interesting and fragile contents of the Special Collections Library's collections, when, in the spring semester of 2011, Sarah Nesbitt, later a MFA graduate in the School of Visual Arts, and Brian Maynard joined the project. Both were students in Professors Kenyon's and Rosas's game classes. They created a digital architecture by using a game production software called Unity that can be used to drop in images of a variety of movable books in order to create an interactive website. Before the students began their work, they requested an instructional session on the history of printing and early books. For all these students, this was the first opportunity they had ever had to be engaged in the history of books and the history of games.

This project gave Special Collections an opportunity to preserve extremely fragile and unique objects that are often used in instructional contexts and to initiate a web-based collection that will be in demand by scholars internationally. This would give technology professionals an opportunity to investigate and implement new solutions. Because of their "movable" character, exploring technology applications where users will be able to mimic the interactive nature of the object and engage with the objects by playing with them virtually would be very helpful. Through the efforts of Professor Jacqueline Reid-Walsh, a scholar of early children's books in Penn State's Department of Education and a recipient of an NEH startup grant "Learning as Playing: An Animated, Interactive Archive of Seventeenth- to Nineteenth-Century Narrative Media for and by Children," it will be possible to help researchers explore the nature of play in earlier children's literature. Professor Reid-Walsh had already successfully enlisted the participation of the curators of children's books at Princeton, Harvard, the Bodleian Library at Oxford, and the British Library. They all expressed willingness to provide digital images of the earliest flap books in their own important collections to add to the Penn State Libraries website.

Please review one example—http://blogs.tlt.psu.edu/projects/flapbook—done as an experiment using Flash to display how a flap book operates. Applications of the technology will be extended to demonstrate how other early toys, including the earliest paper dolls, were manipulated by the players. Eventually, similar examples for toys and games in the collections will be created. These include game boards, architectural building blocks, drawing manuals, interchangeable blocks, and pop-up books. The Allison-Shelley Collection has a special emphasis on toys by Friedrich Fröbel, an important early German educator who designed balls, wooden blocks, tiles, sticks, and metal rings to demonstrate that children learn by playing.

As a Bednar intern, Brian Maynard benefitted from working on an NEH grant–funded project and gained professional experience in working with "clients" such as the University Libraries. In addition to acquiring knowledge of book history from Professor Reid-Walsh and me, he was trained in the handling of rare and fragile materials and spent valuable time with staff from the Digitization and Preservation Department, who provided training on the Betterlight camera. This project was a wonderful opportunity for a student to be engaged in a truly interdisciplinary project in an area of the humanities that has been underexplored in the digital age. He was included by name in the online acknowledgments.

Brian wrote:

As an undergraduate, I am honored to be part of a grant with as much prestige as this. It really feels exciting to be involved in something so much more academic and important than my usual programming and game design studies. Getting the opportunity to see the rare books collection here at Penn State was fairly enlightening to me, as it gave me some perspective on the challenges associated with preserving and even acquiring such artifacts for scholastic study. This particular collection is of interest to me because of its roots in the definitions of 'play' and 'gaming' that the video game industry (and my study towards it) owes its lineage to. I appreciate this great opportunity.

Sarah Nesbitt likewise found it a wonderful experience to have during her last semester at Penn State:

I had been working on my thesis, called *Making Sense of What We Have,* which is based on the fact that written and visual information is and will always be vulnerable to re-interpretation and re-contextualization. Working on this project to produce digital documentation of rare children's books has helped me to become more familiar with a way of preserving a piece of history. With the help of Sandra Stelts, we were provided with a selection of children's books from 1814 and 1833, and with the aid of Albert Rozo and Curt Krebs, I was able to work with the large-format camera to digitally document these books. After I did some post-production editing, I gave the files to Brian Maynard, who turned them into interactive digital media. This has been a great way to make the books more accessible for other educators, children, and students, and still keep the original books preserved. The best part was that because I had to figure out how to document the books, I also had to play with the books themselves in order to discover how they function.

Within the concept of "toys that teach," Professor Reid-Walsh's project has led us all into a greater understanding of our collections. After our class session she wrote, "Gazing at these artifacts and tentatively touching a few under close supervision, we were all drawn into another world from another time. We could gain insight into the culture and the play of 19th-century children in a way that is not possible through reading books alone. As I left the display assembled by Sandra Stelts, looking at the landscape of games and books on the tables reminded me of the importance of studying the material culture of a period, which provides a tangible and visual context for the literature. John Locke, the famous Enlightenment philosopher of childhood, believed that it was possible to play into knowledge and that we learn best by an informed and gentle guide. He would have approved completely of our Special Collections excursion.

Several other internship projects demonstrated the range of activities and some of the longer-term impacts that these opportunities can have on the undergraduates who have worked on them. Brief descriptions of four of these are included here:

- **Erin Dini** was the Bednar in Rare Books and Manuscripts in the Special Collections Library in 2001–2002. Her primary project was to process the papers of Caribbean writer Vivian Virtue (1911–1998) and to create an exhibit on Virtue's life and writings. Erin's finding aid for the collection can be found at http://www.libraries.psu.edu/dam/psul/up/digital/findingaids/2587.htm. After graduating with a major in English, Erin was hired at the Penn State Press as an editorial assistant. She has since earned a library degree at Simmons College in Boston and then worked as the assistant library director at North Logan Public Library, North Logan, Utah. She is now an academic reference librarian at Utah State University in Salt Lake City.
- **Jennifer Slivka** was an English major and a Bednar intern in Rare Books and Manuscripts during the fall of 2002. She processed the LaFayette Butler Collection of Arnold Bennett Publishing Correspondence and Manuscripts, 1903–1931, which included extensive correspondence between Bennett and his agents and publishers. Jennifer became so absorbed in the lives of the correspondents that she came to my office one day and wailed "James Pinker died!" when she read of his death in a letter! Her finding aid to the collection is located at http://resources.libraries.psu.edu/findingaids/2606.htm. Jennifer's first job was in a research position at the American Institutes for Research in Washington, D.C. She is now enrolled at the University of Miami as a graduate student in their Irish Studies program, where she was recently awarded a Dissertation Fellowship from the College of Art and Sciences Center for the Humanities for the spring 2011 semester for her dissertation "Strangers at Home: Threshold Identities in Contemporary Irish Women's Writing."
- **Ali Busacca** was a Bednar intern in Rare Books and Manuscripts in 2006–2007 and worked concurrently as a reporter for the *Daily Collegian*. Her skills as a newspaper writer (which included incredible energy, a respect for deadlines, a clear and precise writing style, and a thorough grounding in the who-what-when-where-why basics of journalism) made her a superb intern for processing literary manuscript collections and writing concise collection descriptions. She left Penn State for New York City to work for an online magazine called *iVillage* and is currently working as a web editor for the *New York Times* Travel section. She also writes a blog at http://allisonbusacca.blogspot.com. About a year ago, she wrote: "I still talk about the Bednar internship. It was such an incredible and interesting experience."
- **Jennifer Dlugosz** was a Bednar intern in 2007–2008, jointly supervised by Karen Dabney, conservator in the Digitization and Preservation Department, and me, the curator of Rare Books and Manuscripts. Her major project was to conduct a survey of our collection of more than 500 sixteenth- and seventeenth-century emblem books and to create a database that enables us to plan for their future preservation and care. She was also involved in many hands-on preservation projects and assisted us in making Mylar covers for dust jackets and handmade boxes for other fragile collections. Jennifer is currently in the art history graduate program at the University of Virginia and working part time at Monticello.

Working with these students will also produce tremendous outcomes for the libraries: in accelerating digital projects, improving access for all users in new interdisciplinary areas, and learning from the students about new technology. As discovered in the brief time spent with the IDS students this semester, staff has as much to learn from *them* as they have to learn from staff, as they give staff technical lessons of opportunity. Being able to render three-dimensional objects and allowing the user to manipulate them could also have significant applications for future digitization projects in the sciences.

CONCLUSION

Working with undergraduates has proved to be a wonderfully satisfying personal experience. These young students have far exceeded expectations with their dogged work in processing challenging manuscript collections, curating exhibitions, and "animating" early books. Lessons learned include discovering that a casual and fortuitous conversation with a student after a class can benefit Special Collections and the student in unexpected ways, providing new experiences of value in the students' chosen careers.

The undergraduate students have been surprisingly sophisticated about literature, scholarship, and technology, and they have consistently produced work at a high level. It is possible to capitalize on their many diverse talents, including graceful writing, foreign language transcription, computer skills in gaming programming, and hands-on, practical knowledge of nineteenth-century photographic processes. A priority will be to continue to explore ways in which students will be captivated by the unique materials and primary sources in Special Collections as staff learn from their fresh approaches to learning and marketing the collections in exciting ways.

8

Engaging International Students with the Academic Library

Dawn Amsberry, Reference and Instruction Librarian,
Penn State University Libraries

INTRODUCTION

In conversations with academic librarians about engaging international students in library initiatives, they make such comments as "we're just beginning to offer special programming for international students and are looking for new ideas" or "we are very interested in working with this population, but we aren't sure how to get started." In academic libraries across the country, there is a growing interest in and even excitement about engaging our overseas students as well as a sense of opportunities for exploring unchartered territory. While international students have attended American college and university campuses for decades, librarians and educators are becoming more acutely aware of the importance of globalization and the subsequent need for a deeper understanding of international cultures. This chapter will describe some of the new ways academic librarians around the country are engaging their international populations and will provide suggestions for implementing programming.

International student enrollment in the United States has grown dramatically since the 1950s and 1960s, when there were fewer than 100,000 overseas students nationwide. Enrollment rose to more than 300,000 in the 1980s and continued a steady climb into the twenty-first century. In the 2009–2010 academic year, there were 690,923 international students enrolled in higher education in the United States, representing 3.5 percent of the total student enrollment. Following a dip in 2003, international student enrollment began to rise again in 2006 and continued its upward climb in 2009, up 2.9 percent over the previous year.

China sends the largest number of students to the United States, followed by India and South Korea. Chinese student enrollment made a leap forward in 2009, up almost 30 percent from the previous year, for a total of 127,628 students, or 18.5 percent of the total international student population. Top fields of study for international students are business and engineering, followed by physical and life sciences, math and computer science, and social sciences (Open Doors 2010).

Academic librarians have been interested in reaching international students since the 1980s, when international student enrollment climbed to 300,000 and librarians began writing about the unique issues facing this population. In an extensive bibliography of nearly 600 resources published between 1940 and 2008, Peters (2010) chronicles the evolving awareness in the academic library field of the importance of developing special services for their international community. While some issues, such as technological barriers, have changed as students around the world develop technical proficiency, other issues, such as language and cultural differences, endure and continue to impact library instruction, reference, and programming. Since 2009, more than 20 articles on international and English as a Second Language (ESL) students and academic libraries have been published in the library literature, indicating the continued interest in exploring this area.

NATIONAL SURVEY OF ACADEMIC LIBRARIES AND INTERNATIONAL STUDENTS

In fall 2010, an 18-question survey on academic library services to international students was distributed to institutions around the country via multiple professional library listservs. The survey questions are included in Appendix A. The following section will describe the general results of the survey. The survey responses are not meant to be indicative of national trends; rather, they will be used to highlight specific initiatives that may be of interest to libraries wishing to expand their offerings for international students. Responses from 47 institutions in 28 states were received. Of the responding institutions, 26 were universities, 13 were four-year colleges, 5 were two-year colleges, and the remaining 3 classified themselves as "other." The majority of the institutions were small to midsized: 34 had a student enrollment of 10,000 or less and only 4 respondents indicated an enrollment of more than 30,000. The international student enrollment for most of the reporting institutions was also fairly small, with 25 respondents reporting an international student population of 300 or less. Only two institutions had more than 5,000 international students. The institutional data from the survey is summarized in Table 8.1.

Table 8.1

Responding Institutions by Type, Total Student Enrollment, and International Student Enrollment

Institution Type		Student Enrollment		International Student Enrollment	
University	26	0–5,000	26	0–300	25
4-year	13	5,000–10,000	8	300–500	6
2-year	5	10,000–20,000	4	500–1,000	3
Other	3	20,000–30,000	5	1,000–3,000	8
		30,000–40,000	4	3,000–5,000	3
		40,000+	0	5,000+	2

Although data on percentages of international students as a portion of the total student enrollment were not specifically collected on the survey, the size of the overall student population at the institution generally correlated with the number of international students ($\rho_{45} = 0.75$, $p < 0.0001$) as reported in these questions. However, a search of *The College Blue Book* (2009) indicates that 38 of the 47 responding schools, including all 9 schools with more than 20,000 students, have an international student enrollment of 5 percent or less of the total student population. The four schools with an international student enrollment of more than 10 percent were smaller institutions with a total student population of 20,000 or less. This suggest that while larger institutions usually have larger numbers of international students, they do not necessarily have a greater ratio of international students and that all institutions, not just those with large student enrollments, should be aware of the percentage of international students on their campuses and develop services accordingly.

In addition to information about their institutions, survey respondents were asked about services and programs currently offered for international students. The answers to these questions are summarized in Table 8.2. More than half (57%) of the institutions offer an orientation for new international students, which is separate from orientations for other incoming students. Of those librarians who do offer a special international student orientation, 24 indicated that they include a general introduction to library services and 18 librarians include a library tour. Five institutions, four of which are large universities with more than 20,000 students, include an orientation to subject libraries or specific disciplines.

When asked if they offer special programming for international students other than orientations, 40 percent of respondents indicated that they do. Eleven libraries offer international-themed book displays, including displays showcasing specific countries, while seven include cultural programming. Other types of international-related programming cited were guest speakers, contests, and workshops. One respondent noted that "the library actively supports events with a cultural awareness theme, often cosponsoring those events to be held in the library."

In regards to promoting services, 36 percent of respondents indicated that they market their regular services (such as reference, research consultation, etc.) specifically

Table 8.2
Summary of Numbers of Libraries with Services to International Students

General Orientation	27
General Orientation with Tour	18
Subject Library Orientation	5
Special Programs	19
International-Themed Book Displays	11
Promotion of Regular Services (reference, research consultation, etc.)	17
Print Publications (guides, brochures, etc.) in English	5
Liaisons	9
Website	4
Multilingual Services and Materials	7
Staff Training	5

to international students. The campus office for international students was the most popular outlet for promotion (11 respondents), followed by ESL classes and international student clubs. In response to other questions related to outreach and promotion initiatives, five respondents said they provide print publications, such as guides and brochures, specifically for international students, nine said they have a librarian designated as a liaison to international students, and four have international student webpages. One respondent noted that a webpage for international students was currently under development.

Seven librarians in this survey—all working in larger universities—indicated that they offer their services or materials in languages other than English. A few librarians provide tours (both in person and recorded) as well as reference, instruction, and printed guides and handouts in other languages, while one institution has a multilingual webpage. One survey participant explained that although her library does not provide regular tours or programming in non-English languages, those services are available upon request. The most popular language mentioned was Spanish (five respondents), followed by Chinese, Korean, and Japanese. Other languages mentioned were Hmong, French, and Bulgarian.

In response to a question about staff training, only five respondents indicated that they currently offer training for staff on issues related to international students, such as cross-cultural awareness. Two respondents mentioned informal training, such as discussions among colleagues about "ways to reach international students and to understand the cultural patterns behind their questions." One survey participant identified training on cross-cultural awareness as a specific interest, although such training was not currently in place. These results suggest an interest in and a need for more training programs in academic libraries addressing the needs of international students. Some specific suggestions for training are discussed later in this chapter.

It is clear from the foregoing discussion that many academic librarians are exploring programs and services for international students, although the extent and type of these initiatives vary widely. Individual comments from participants suggest an enthusiasm for working with their international patrons. Two survey respondents indicated that reading the survey questions gave them new insight into what they could be doing to address the unique educational needs of international students. The following section will highlight some of the specific programming mentioned in the comments section of the survey as well as initiatives I have been engaged in and have heard about through discussions with other academic librarians.

THE PERSONAL TOUCH: ORIENTATIONS AND LIAISONS

The survey results show that an international student library orientation is a popular way of reaching incoming students. Approaches to the orientation vary; some librarians make their orientation a social event with refreshments, while others focus on orienting students to library resources and services. At Penn State, where the overall student population at the University Park campus is 44,000 and the international students number more than 4,000, librarians in the University Libraries offer an orientation for incoming international students in the fall and in the spring. The fall orientation, which is when most new students come to campus, usually draws more than 100 students, while the spring offering is much smaller, typically drawing 30 to 50 students, reflecting the smaller size of the incoming spring class.

The orientation originally consisted of a general introduction to library services with refreshments; however, because most of our international students begin their studies with their major or discipline already defined, the event was expanded to include tours and orientations by library subject specialists. Following the general introductory portion, the students are divided into groups according to discipline and taken to one of nine subject-specific libraries. In a survey conducted during the Fall 2010 orientation, students rated the subject library portion of the orientation very highly, mentioning the importance of finding "my librarian" or "my subject area." One student commented, "It was excellent that we received a personalized subject-specific orientation."

While orientations are an effective way to get students into the library, they often occur at a time when international students are in the midst of adjusting to enormous changes. During informal focus groups conducted with international students at Penn State, several students mentioned that their first few weeks on campus were overwhelming, and although they attended the library orientation, they did not retain much of the information presented. One student found the sheer physical size of our building daunting, commenting that "the aisles and rooms and ways and paths are just too many and are confusing." These comments, coupled with the comments from students about the importance of meeting their librarian, suggest that orientations should emphasize people while minimizing myriad details of library services and collections that will not be retained.

A colorful one-page handout or postcard with key information and perhaps the URL of a webpage for international students can provide students with a starting place for further exploration on their own at a later, less hectic time. For example, at the DiMenna-Nyselius Library at Fairfield University, students receive a one-page handout that summarizes the information covered in the orientation and includes a link to an online guide for international students (DiMenna-Nyselius Library 2011).

As a way to emphasize the friendly face of the library without overwhelming new students, some librarians have liaison or personal librarian programs. Librarians at the University of Massachusetts, Amherst Libraries, distribute their cards at the general campus orientation for international students and introduce themselves as "your personal librarian"—available to help with general library questions and to refer students to the appropriate subject specialist for research questions. At the DiMenna-Nyselius Library at Fairfield University, the personal librarian for international students sends e-mails to all international students once a month to promote services and ongoing events and also meets with them for research help. Of the institutions in the survey who indicated that they had liaison librarians for international students, four were large universities with an enrollment of more than 20,000 students; however, three smaller universities and two community colleges with fewer than 1,000 international students also have liaisons, indicating that this type of service can be implemented in a variety of settings.

Librarians who engage in these liaison and outreach roles are likely to have a personal interest in working with international students—perhaps because they are internationals themselves, they are multilingual and enjoy using their language skills, they may have been former ESL teachers, or they simply have an interest in language and culture. This personal interest is critical to engaging international students and was revealed repeatedly in the national survey: one respondent advises the campus International Club, and several participate in their institution's international host family program. At Penn State, librarians have volunteered as conversation partners for internationals through a local community-based nonprofit organization.

BEYOND THE LIBRARY WALLS: PARTNERSHIPS WITH OTHER CAMPUS UNITS

Librarians can work toward engaging international students by moving beyond the library walls to develop partnerships with other units on campus. Not only do such external collaborations assist students, but they also result in increased campus visibility for the library (Love and Edwards 2009). As discussed above, the results of the national survey indicate that the campus office for international students is an excellent resource for promoting the library. This office works directly with students on a regular basis and may offer ongoing programming, such as a monthly coffee hour, where librarians can hand out promotional literature or even make an informal presentation.

At Penn State, the librarians coordinate the international student library orientation with the Office of Global Programs as part of the larger orientation for all incoming international students. The Office of Global Programs also publishes an online weekly newsletter, written and edited by these international students, providing an ideal avenue for publicizing library events. Other opportunities for collaboration include cosponsoring guest speakers, displays, or other programming for International Education Week, a national event that takes place each year during the third week of November. ESL classes are also a popular means of reaching international students.

Many colleges and universities have an intensive English program for nondegree students who want to improve their English before going on to higher education in the United States. These students can benefit greatly from a library instruction session—not only because it will help them prepare for their future studies but also because it provides them with an opportunity to practice their listening and speaking skills in English. Matriculated international students may also be required to take an ESL class in academic writing.

To reach the students in these courses at Penn State, the course instructors—many of whom are international graduate students themselves—are invited to an informational lunch, at which the library's instructional services for their students as well as library resources they could use in their own graduate studies are discussed. This initiative has resulted in an increase in the number of ESL instructors requesting library instruction sessions.

Although many international students can be reached through ESL classes, not all students from abroad take these classes, which are designed only for those students who do not speak English as a first language. Students from India, who make up about 18 percent of the current total international student population in the United States, often speak English as one of their first languages and therefore are not required to complete ESL classes. Other students have gained fluency in other venues and are placed in the regular classes. These students, then, must be reached through other means, such as international student clubs. Penn State has dozens of international student clubs representing various countries and nationalities, including an Indian Graduate Student Association and a South Asian Student Association as well as the International Student Council. Student club members can be invited to give a presentation about their culture or religion at the library or a librarian could offer to visit the club's meeting as a guest speaker.

PEER-TO-PEER ENGAGEMENT: INTERNATIONAL STUDENTS AS THE FACE OF THE LIBRARY

In the national survey discussed in this chapter, one respondent commented, "Our library hires international students, so many of them are able to help other international students." Students are often more comfortable consulting a peer than they are approaching a librarian; the same is true for international students, who may be even more likely to approach someone from their own country or region. A library assistant from India told me that she is often approached by Indian students in the library, particularly those who have just recently arrived on campus and are looking for a friendly face.

In addition to employing international students at public service desks, librarians can also engage international students to work on special projects as interns—either paid or for course credit. Internships can provide international students with practical experience in writing and translating, promoting programs, developing collections, or creating computer applications. An internship can be an ideal way for international students to share their cultural backgrounds with other students, through translating a library tour into other languages, recommending popular book titles published overseas, or organizing international-themed library events.

At University Libraries, two Chinese-speaking international students were hired. They each completed a semester-long paid internship, for which they also received course credit through the College of Liberal Arts internship program. The students were selected in part because of their language abilities, and one of their major projects was to translate and record an audio tour of the library in Mandarin Chinese, which is now available on our website as a podcast (Penn State University Libraries 2010). Although eventually it would be good to provide audio tours in many languages, for this initial effort, focus was on Chinese because Chinese-speakers make up the largest portion of international students at Penn State, constituting about 21 percent of the overall international student body.

In addition to their language skills, the interns also made use of their cultural knowledge in developing a list of popular books in Chinese recommended for the leisure reading collection. During informal focus groups with international students at Penn State, several students suggested expanding the library's collection to include popular books from overseas in their original languages, and the interns also showed great enthusiasm for this project. One of the interns was excited to be able to put her love of Chinese novels to good use and liked the idea of other students benefitting from her knowledge. As she put it, "I thought it would be a great idea for Chinese students to have something in their own language that they could read for fun."

The interns worked very independently on these projects, bringing their own expertise and creativity to their work. They also contributed to a number of other projects, including translating a welcome letter for students into Chinese and publicizing library events through Chinese Facebook and Twitter posts. The students valued these opportunities to share their cultural and linguistic knowledge as well as the chance to use their initiative and creativity. One of the interns commented: "I have really enjoyed this internship mostly because of the space I was given to be creative in completing all the projects." The other intern expressed a similar sentiment: "This internship experience allowed me to complete different projects according to what I thought I should do and at my own pace."

International students need not be employed at library public service desks or even as interns in order to share their expertise. Downing and Klein (2001) describe a project in which students were hired on a contract basis to translate the English-language script for a virtual library tour into their native languages. The translators were recruited through campus cultural organizations, helping librarians develop stronger ties with these groups. To ensure the quality of the translation, two translators worked on each tour and compared results; the work was then reviewed by at least one translator/editor. Although the student translators were paid a nominal fee for their work, they contributed additional hours of their own time because of "the strong sense of pride they felt in being included in the project." Because of this personal pride in contributing their skills, students may be willing to volunteer their time toward translation projects. The Paul V. Galvin Library at the Illinois Institute of Technology provides video tours in several languages on its website and invites student volunteers to help with creating additional tours (Paul V. Galvin Library 2011).

TRANSLATING THE LIBRARY: MULTILINGUAL SERVICES

The initiatives described earlier involve providing international students with materials in their native languages. However, at a recent ALA discussion group among academic librarians, several participants noted that on their campuses, providing multilingual services and materials to international students was controversial, even frowned upon, because students were expected to conduct most of their academic communication in English. In the survey discussed in this chapter, most respondents indicated that their libraries did not provide services or materials in languages other than English, although the reasons for this could be myriad, including lack of funding and staff time to devote to translation projects. A few respondents did indicate that they offer services and materials in other languages; for example, the Paul V. Galvin Library at the Illinois Institute of Technology provides research guides, tutorials, and in-person research help in Chinese.

The questions then arises, do international students want or need library services and materials in their native languages? In a study by Jackson (2005), students repeatedly asked for more materials in other languages, particularly daily newspapers from their home countries. In focus groups conducted with international students at Penn State, several participants indicated an interest in popular reading titles in their native languages, such as novels published in their home countries. On the other hand, a study of international students and language preference (Ferrer-Vinent 2010) found that a large majority of respondents (83%) preferred to use English at the reference desk. This evidence may indicate that while international students want to read materials in their native languages for their own enjoyment and learning, they prefer to communicate and conduct library business in English.

International students are generally required to demonstrate a high level of proficiency in English before acceptance into American colleges and universities, and many overseas students speak English fluently as one of their first languages. International students will need to conduct their coursework, research, academic communication, and much of their personal business largely in English during their stay in the United States. However, even students proficient in English may feel welcomed and comforted by library signs, publications, and collections in their native languages, particularly during their first weeks and months on campus. Multilingual materials, then, can serve to welcome students to the library, providing them with a piece of home in their new environment.

Even if librarians are not able to provide materials in their students' home languages, international students can also be reached and welcomed through materials in English targeted toward their needs. A colorful postcard or brochure featuring photos of international students in the library can be distributed at orientations, through the international student office, and to ESL classes. Such materials can highlight services or collections of particular interest to international students, such as international newspapers or popular foreign language titles. Publicity for international students can also emphasize services the students may not be aware of, such as the "Ask a Librarian" chat reference, or research consultation appointments with subject specialists, as these services may not be provided in the students' home country libraries.

Even the most proficient second-language speakers may not be familiar with American idioms and slang, and such usage should be avoided or explained in written and oral communication with international students. After a presentation given to new international scholars and faculty, one scholar asked to see the "branch library" on the campus map, indicating that this particular usage of the word "branch" was new to her. An explanation of the tree trunk/branch analogy brought a delighted smile to her face. Likewise, avoid library jargon that can elicit puzzled frowns or blank looks even among American students. For example, many students assume that the term "holdings" in the catalog refers to books that are "on hold." For translating and explaining library vocabulary, the *ACRL Instruction Section's Multilingual Glossary* (ACRL 2008), which includes library terms translated into six languages as well as definitions of terms in English, is a very useful tool.

STAFF TRAINING: RAISING CROSS-CULTURAL AWARENESS

Innovative library programs and services for international students, such as those described earlier, will not be successful without the support of librarians and staff. Before beginning initiatives for engaging students, librarians in managerial positions may need to look at ways to train staff to work more effectively with a diverse student population. Workshops on cross-cultural awareness, led by knowledgeable librarians or by faculty experts from the institution's academic departments, can help heighten sensitivity about the issues faced by students from other cultures. International students themselves can be invited to contribute to sensitivity training by describing their own experiences adjusting to a new culture during panel presentations for library faculty and staff. As noted by Berlanga-Cortéz (2000), cross-cultural training involves increasing awareness about cultural differences as well as identifying our own assumptions about other cultural groups.

Suggestions for elements to include in training workshops can be garnered from the library literature. Osa, Nyana, and Ogbaa (2006) provide a list of tips for enhancing reference services with international patrons, including respecting cross-cultural rules about personal space, being aware of nonverbal communication, and avoiding humor that might be misinterpreted. These authors also suggest asking students to write down words or phrases that are not being understood because students may be more comfortable with written communication than with speaking English aloud. Berlanga-Cortéz (2000) recommends training staff to be aware of differences in communication style; for example, quiet behavior exhibited by some international students may signify respect for authority rather than shyness or a lack of understanding. Amsberry (2009) gives suggestions for improving listening skills when working with ESL speakers, such as listening for meaning rather than individual sounds and being aware of one's own attitude toward accented speech.

CONCLUSION

As this chapter illustrates, academic librarians are finding new and innovative ways to engage their growing international student population. The following list summarizes many of the best ideas discussed in this chapter. No library can be expected to implement all of them; the list is meant as a menu from which to choose the most appropriate recommendations for any given library and circumstance.

- Offer a library orientation for new international students that emphasizes getting to know librarians.
- When possible and appropriate, incorporate subject specialist librarians and subject libraries into the orientation.
- Designate one or more librarians as liaisons to international students.
- Develop partnerships with the international student office and with international student clubs and organizations.
- Make connections with ESL instructors to encourage requests for library instruction for ESL classes.
- Hire international students for library public service positions.
- Engage international students in library projects as interns or volunteers or on a contract basis.
- Expand library collections of popular reading material in other languages.
- Create a postcard or brochure to market library services to international students.
- Develop a website for international students.
- Organize international-themed events and displays.
- In oral and written communication with ESL speakers, eliminate or explain idioms, slang, and library jargon.
- To help librarians and staff engage more fully with international students, provide training sessions on cross-cultural communication issues.

Expanding library services to international students benefits not only the students themselves but also the library as a whole by strengthening partnerships with other campus units, raising library staff awareness of cross-cultural issues, and possibly even broadening the worldview of other library patrons. As society becomes increasingly internationalized, academic libraries can play a key role in the globalization of their campuses and in the ongoing development of global citizens.

REFERENCES

ACRL Instruction Section. "Multilingual Glossary." ACRL (2008), http://www.ala.org/acrl/about acrl/directoryofleadership/sections/is/iswebsite/projpubs/multilingual.

Amsberry, Dawn. "Using Effective Listening Skills with International Patrons." *Reference Services Review* 37, no. 1 (2009): 10–19.

Berlanga-Cortéz, Graciela. "Cross-Cultural Communication: Identifying Barriers to Information Retrieval with Culturally and Linguistically Different Library Patrons." In *Library Services*

to Latinos: An Anthology, edited by Salvador Güereña, 51–60. Jefferson, NC: McFarland, 2000.
The College Blue Book. 36th ed. Detroit: Macmillan Reference, 2009.
DiMenna-Nyselius Library. "International Student Library Orientation." Fairfield University (2011), http://librarybestbets.fairfield.edu/content.php?pid=140476&sid=1250500.
Downing, Arthur, and Leo Robert Klein. "A Multilingual Virtual Tour for International Students: The Web-Based Library at Baruch College Opens Doors." *College & Research Libraries News* 62, no. 5 (2001): 500–502.
Ferrer-Vinent, Ignacio. "For English, Press 1: International Students' Language Preference at the Reference Desk." *The Reference Librarian* 51, no. 3 (2010): 189–201. doi:10.1080/02763871003800429.
Jackson, Pamela A. "Incoming International Students and the Library: A Survey." *Reference Services Review* 33, no. 2 (2005): 197–209. doi:10.1108/00907320510597408.
Love, Emily, and Margaret B. Edwards. "Forging Inroads between Libraries and Academic, Multicultural and Student Services." *Reference Services Review* 37, no. 1 (2009): 20–29. doi:10.1108/00907320910934968.
Open Doors. "Open Doors 2010 Fast Facts." Institute of International Education (2010), http://www.iie.org/en/Research-and-Publications/Open-Doors.
Osa, Justin O., Sylvia A. Nyana, and Clara A. Ogbaa. "Effective Cross-Cultural Communication to Enhance Reference Transactions: Training Guidelines and Tips." *Knowledge Quest* 35, no. 2 (2006): 22–24.
Paul V. Galvin Library. "Multilingual Library Virtual Tour." Illinois Institute of Technology (2011), http://guides.library.iit.edu/content.php?pid=173230&sid=1457541&search_terms=tour.
Penn State University Libraries. "University Libraries Tours." Penn State (2010), http://www.libraries.psu.edu/psul/lls/outreach/tours.html.
Peters, Diane E. *International Students and Academic Libraries: A Survey of Issues and Annotated Bibliography.* Lanham, MD: Scarecrow Press, 2010.

APPENDIX A: SURVEY QUESTIONS

Library Services for International Students

General Information

For the purposes of this survey, international students are defined as students who are not U.S. citizens or U.S. permanent residents.

1. What is the name of your institution?
   _____

2. What is the type of your institution?
   ___ Two-year college
   ___ Four-year college
   ___ University
   ___ Other, please specify

3. What is the approximate total student population at your institution?
   ___ 0–5,000
   ___ 5,000–10,000
   ___ 10,000–20,000
   ___ 20,000–30,000

___ 30,000–40,000
___ Over 40,000
4. What is the approximate international student population at your institution?
___ 0–300
___ 300–500
___ 500–1,000
___ 1,000–3,000
___ 3,000–5,000
___ Over 5,000

Programs and Services

5. Does your library offer orientations for new international students (separate from orientations for other incoming students)?
___ Yes
___ No
6. If you answered yes to question 5, do the orientations for international students include any of the following? Check all that apply.
___ General tour of the library
___ General introduction to library services
___ Tours and/or orientations to subject libraries or specific disciplines
___ Other, please specify
7. Does your library offer any of the following special programming (other than orientations) for international students? Check all that apply.
___ Cultural programs
___ Guest speakers
___ Displays
___ Contests
___ Workshops
___ None of the above
___ Other, please specify

Outreach and Marketing

8. Does your library promote its regular services (such as reference, research consultation, etc.) specifically to international students?
___ Yes
___ No
9. If you answered yes to question 8, where do you promote these services to international students? Check all that apply.
___ International student clubs
___ English as a Second Language classes
___ Campus office for international students
___ Campus housing for international students
___ Other, please specify
10. Does your library provide print publications (such as guides, brochures, etc.) targeted specifically toward international students?
___ Yes
___ No

11. Does your library have a librarian officially designated as the liaison to international students?
    ___ Yes
    ___ No
12. Does your library have a webpage specifically for international students?
    ___ Yes
    ___ No

Multilingual Services

13. Does your library provide services or printed materials (such as library guides or handouts) in languages other than English?
    ___ Yes
    ___ No
14. If you answered yes to question 13, does your library provide any of the following services or materials in languages other than English? Check all that apply.
    ___ In-person tours
    ___ Virtual, audio, or video tours
    ___ Reference assistance
    ___ Instruction
    ___ Printed guides, brochures or handouts
    ___ Webpages
    ___ Other, please specify
15. In which languages are the services and materials listed in question 14 provided? Check all that apply.
    ___ Chinese
    ___ Spanish
    ___ Korean
    ___ Japanese
    ___ Other, please specify

Staff Training

16. Does your library offer training for staff on issues related to international students, such as cross-cultural awareness?
    ___ Yes
    ___ No

Additional Comments

17. Please add any additional comments you would to like to share about your library's initiatives for international students.
    _____
18. If you have special programming for international students and are willing to be credited with best case examples, please provide your contact information (name, institution, and e-mail). Names of institutions will be included in the study only with permission.
    _____

9

Service Learning: Engaging College Students with the Library and Information Literacy Competencies

Maureen Barry, Librarian for First-Year and Distance Learning Services, Wright State University

"Service, combined with learning, adds value to each and transforms both."
—Ellen Porter Honnet and Susan J. Poulsen

INTRODUCTION

This chapter explores the ways in which service-learning pedagogy, when integrated into a credit-bearing information literacy (IL) course, enhances student engagement with the community, the library, and IL competencies. After defining service learning and describing the service-learning IL course model, I will use evidence from students' reflection assignments to demonstrate their engagement with the community, library resources, and IL competencies.

Service learning is defined by the National Service-Learning Clearinghouse as "a teaching and learning strategy that integrates meaningful community service with instruction and reflection to enrich the learning experience, teach civic responsibility, and strengthen communities." Service learning is not synonymous with community service in that it "is a structured learning process" (Burns 1998, 39). Civic engagement, including service learning, is a growing trend in higher education. According to Campus Compact's 2010 Member Survey Executive Report, the percentage of faculty teaching service-learning courses per campus has remained steady over the past few years—between 6 and 7 percent; however, the average number of courses offered per campus has grown from 43 in 2008 to 64 in 2010 (3). The increase in the average number of courses taught is not surprising considering the outcomes described in the education literature. Not only do students understand a subject matter better when it is connected to service learning (Eyler and Giles 1999), but also, according to Kuh, service learning is a high-impact educational practice that improves student retention and student engagement (2008, 9). However, there is little evidence in the literature that librarians are participating in this high-impact practice.

Despite infrequently discussed connections between IL and service-learning pedagogy, some that have written on the subject refer to engagement. Riddle argues that IL can enhance service-learning pedagogy to form engaged models of library instruction (2003, 71). Likewise, Herther considers how service learning can increase student engagement with the academic library as she points out that service-learning partnerships provide opportunities for libraries and librarians to be placed in a social context (2008, 388). Herther also writes that service learning provides an opportunity to expand librarians' interactions with students beyond one-shot classes or brief encounters at library service points, but she warns that these collaborations can be more time intensive (2008, 389). Service-learning collaborations can help position librarians as more than guardians of books in the user's mind. These meaningful interactions supplied by service-learning partnerships with faculty, students, and community partners are worth the time invested. For example, some service-learning experiences may require somewhat unique information compared with typical research paper assignments. Thus, librarians can situate themselves as partners to help faculty and students find information and local data surrounding the social issues the community partners strive to solve (Riddle 2003, 75). Few practical examples of such partnerships have been documented in the literature. In both projects, librarians partnered with faculty who teach service-learning courses in their respective disciplines and helped students research issues or policies related to their community partners (Nutefall 2009; Hernandez and Knight 2010). In this chapter, the author describes student engagement with the community, the library, and IL competencies in a service-learning IL course.

EDT 110: COMMUNITY RESEARCH CONNECTIONS

In 2008, coinstructor Cheryl Lauricella and I proposed an IL course that would incorporate service learning. One of the primary motivations for integrating service learning was the assumption that students retain course material better when it is tied to real-world issues. Wright State University's director of service learning assisted by participating in initial meetings with the community partner to ensure a mutually beneficial experience for the institution and the community agency.

The course—EDT 110: Community Research Connections—and its syllabus and assignments require students to develop IL competencies as they find, select, evaluate, and synthesize information for the community partners: Children's Hunger Alliance and Project READ. Agency staff members then use the sources to inform decision making, implement new programs, write grants, or educate their volunteers and clients (Barry 2011, 347). Since 2008, students have compiled research portfolios made up of annotated bibliographies for the two community partners. In doing so, students gather information that is instrumental to helping solve problems related to hunger and literacy in the region. The instructors' intuitions regarding greater engagement with library resources and IL competencies have been confirmed, as will be discussed later in this chapter. In order to understand student engagement and other course outcomes, it is important to establish the framework for the EDT110 course.

Instructors typically spend the first four classes introducing content (e.g., the invisible web, database demonstrations, keyword generation, information cycle, etc.). They craft homework assignments that provide opportunities for students to practice the skills they learned in class and find resources for Project READ. For example, the first two homework assignments require students to submit three websites and three articles about their research topic. The instructors review these sources and, if necessary, suggest other keywords with which the students can search to find more appropriate sources.

Students work together in small groups during the last three or four class periods to select the most appropriate sources, remove duplicate sources found during previous individual homework assignments, and complete citations and annotations. Because all group work is done in class, instructors regularly provide feedback to help students refine their search strategies as they learn to be more effective and efficient searchers. Each homework assignment builds on the last until the students complete their research portfolios.

Although most research portfolios tend to come together nicely in the end, instructors and students experience some challenges along the way. For example, several groups in previous EDT 110 sections experienced a lot of frustration when trying to plan meetings outside of class, which sometimes led to excessive group conflict. When the instructors attended a team-based learning workshop, they were given some strategies to improve group dynamics. Based on the recommendations of team-based learning experts (Michealson, Knight, and Fink 2004), instructors arranged the syllabus such that all group work took place in class. Students no longer had the hassle of finding common meeting times, and their individual homework assignments contributed to the final group research portfolio. As a result, students experienced more success and less frustration with group work. This strategy also improved class attendance overall.

Instructors observed that students have not yet been exposed to scholarly literature, and therefore, they often struggled to identify whether a specific article appropriately addressed the topic at hand. Instructors and students analyzed a few scholarly articles together in class. They used the CRAAP Test, developed at California State University at Chico's Meriam Library, to guide discussion about specific articles and websites.

Lastly, instructors added a new component to the research portfolio during the most recent course in an effort to help students synthesize the information they found. They required students to write recommendations based on the research they gathered. Students did not understand the difference between writing an annotation and writing a recommendation. Due to the time constraints of the two-credit-hour course, instructors will revise this part of the assignment to decrease the level of confusion among students. One way to accomplish this is to ask students such questions as "The author's thesis is _____" and "The methodology used is_____." This exercise can guide students to summarize sources appropriately for annotations. Instructors could also devise a similar exercise to help guide students to write useful recommendations.

Because each homework and in-class assignment is tied to creating the research portfolios, students apply the IL skills they practice to solving real-world issues through the community partnership. Other course-specific details and how the service-learning experiences tie to IL competencies are outlined in *College & Research Libraries News* (Barry 2011).

REFLECTION AS PROOF OF ENGAGEMENT

Reflection is an integral part of any service-learning experience because it supplies a bridge between the service experience and the course content (Bringle and Hatcher 1999, 112). As such, instructors assign reflection papers throughout the quarter to tie service and learning together and to prepare the students to share some of their thoughts during the oral group reflection that takes place on the last day of class. Instructors craft questions that encourage students to consider what skills they acquired in the course as well as what they learned about themselves. Some examples include:

- "What have you learned about your community?"
- "How have your attitudes about research changed as a result of this class?"
- "How have you become a different library user because of this course?"

Community Engagement

A number of students extend beyond their comfort zones during service-learning experiences by putting themselves in another's shoes. According to Eyler and Giles, service-learning outcomes include a reduction of negative stereotypes and increased tolerance toward others (1999, 29). EDT 110 student reactions support this claim. They demonstrate significant personal development during their service-learning experience. Instructors prompt students to think about their own personal growth by asking such questions as "How has your picture of hunger [or literacy] in our community changed because of this class?" or "What did you learn about yourself and your community?" Student comments include:

- "It makes me want to get out and help my community more than ever."
- "Before EDT 110 I thought of hunger as a problem that existed in big cities with adults who did not work and chose not to provide for themselves. I no longer believe that hunger and food insecurity is due to laziness. After seeing the process people have to go through to get food stamps I understand why people cannot do it."

In any service-learning course, involving the community in the classroom lends itself to some uncertainties. Some service-learning students worry about these uncertainties, while others readily welcome the real-world application of course concepts. One EDT 110 student summarized the latter when she said: "You can read something in a textbook, but you can learn so much more when you step into someone else's shoes." A common theme in the preservice reflection writing assignments is that students are nervous about going somewhere unfamiliar. Another student admitted that when he realized on the first day of class that EDT 110 was a service-learning class, he feared that the course would be a lot of work and little return. Part of the service-learning experience is that students learn to adapt to uncertainty just as they will need to throughout life. Most of them had positive experiences as they assisted Children's Hunger Alliance staff members to teach children how to make healthy, inexpensive snacks at a summer 2008 nutrition program. One student wrote:

I did like the volunteer aspect of this class. It was nice to not just be sitting behind a computer the whole time and to get a sense of the children our research is hopefully going to help someday. I used to be big into volunteering, but then "life" takes over and you find a million excuses for why you don't have the time to volunteer. This kind of reminded me about the reason I enjoy helping others, and I hope to become more active with some of my volunteer passions again in the future.

While most on-site service experiences are positive, circumstances beyond the control of instructors or agency partners can cause frustration. For example, Project READ could not host students at a book-sorting service activity as originally planned due to unforeseen circumstances experienced by their book benefactor. Instructors adapted quickly late in the quarter to assign a new service project, during which students educated friends and family about Project READ and literacy needs in the surrounding communities. As students told friends, family, and coworkers about the community partner and the work they do to improve literacy, they also collected small monetary donations to give to the agency. The purpose of this assignment was twofold: first, students felt connected to the agency and its clients; and second, they raised awareness of literacy issues in their community.

The overall positive tone of the group reflection was proof that the students still felt a meaningful connection to Project READ and its clients despite the cancelation of the scheduled on-site service. As they reflected on this aspect of their service-learning experience, they recounted their most meaningful interactions. One appreciated a moment he shared with his mother, during which she told him that she was proud of him for helping the community partner. A few other students said their friends expressed interest in volunteering to be a tutor. Raising awareness of literacy issues in our community is important. This exposure plants a seed among potential volunteers. EDT 110 students and the people they educated about Project READ's work may contribute to the cause in the future by volunteering, donating money, or voting in favor of literacy efforts.

Community partner agency staff and the WSU director of service learning attend the last day of class to take part in an oral reflection activity. Group reflection after the service-learning experience is often powerful. The small class size—8–12 students on average—allows for meaningful discussion, even though they appear to be nervous about sharing their thoughts aloud. The students write a reflection paper before the group reflection, and instructors ask them to be prepared to share at least one observation or thought. The conversation is often slow to start, but the end result is typically significant because students learn from each other and develop a sense of accomplishment. In fact, instructors observe that students often make more meaningful comments during group reflection than they write in their individual reflections, particularly regarding their civic-mindedness and community engagement. This evidence from EDT 110 supports Eyler's claim that when students present conclusions based on shared service-learning experiences, the result is a more compelling conversation than the average student presentation in a typical class (2002, 530).

The instructors discovered that students experience a deeper connection between their work and the community when agency staff members participate in group reflection. During the most recent course, which focused on literacy issues, Project READ's director helped students understand their clients better. For example, she admitted she is still surprised when she hears a child ask "Do I really get to keep this?" even though her agency has given away thousands of books in the Dayton community.

Instructors prompted students to participate in this particular conversation by asking: "Because of your participation in this class, you know that there are kids in your own community that don't even own a book. How might giving a book to a child who doesn't own any affect him or her?" One student responded: "Children are always looking to family for encouragement, and having books in the home could influence children to get praise from their family and share family time to form stronger relationships." Similarly, other students recounted the bonds they experienced as children reading aloud with their parents, and some articulated that they realized that others may never have read with their parents or caregivers. In so doing, they attempted to understand how another person's childhood may have differed from their own.

The students continued to put themselves in another's shoes as one imagined aloud how difficult it would be for an adult to participate in society if he or she cannot read well enough to fill out forms. Another student shared her experiences as a child with a learning disability, and she imagined that she may not be one-quarter away from her college graduation if her parents had not read with her every day.

While reflection assignments encourage students to think about their personal growth and how they engage with their community, they simultaneously prompt them to contemplate what they have learned about the library and the research process. The emerging themes that come from student's reflection activities include confidence in their research abilities, the development of specific skills (such as keyword generation), citing sources and writing annotations, the acknowledgement of the need to evaluate information, and the awareness of subscription-based resources. Each of these themes is discussed in more detail in the following sections.

Library Engagement

After spending nearly 20 hours in the classroom during the 10-week quarter, a majority of EDT 110 students wrote that they experience less frustration during the research process and that their comfort with conducting research increases tremendously. This is evident based on the following statements:

- "Because I now feel more confident in my research skills, I find researching more enjoyable."
- "As a result of this class, I feel much better about doing research in the future, and I do not feel as though I will be overwhelmed by the process anymore."
- "EDT has definitely helped me as an all-around student, and I will use the skills I have learned for many years to come."
- "Completing the research allowed me to become more confident in my ability to do research."

Of course, confidence does not necessarily equate to skill mastery. One of the arguments that Graham and Metaxas make is that a student's confidence in "his or her ability to effectively search the Internet does not significantly affect the students' performance" (2003, 75). However, the instructors hope that confidence and comfort may make the students more likely to apply skills they acquired in EDT 110. Because students in service-learning courses often say they learn to apply course content to other circumstances (Pascarella and Terenzini 2005, 129), instructors feel confident that EDT 110 students use the Internet more cautiously after they complete the course. By the same token, students are more likely to turn to the library for research.

A few students indicated that they feel less intimidated by the size and organization of their campus library. One, in particular, admitted:

I have never found a book in the Wright State Library before this class. I have been to my local library plenty of times, but the University library always intimidated me. In this course, we looked up a book in the library catalog and then actually went to the third floor to find it. Learning where and how to find books will be very useful for my college research later on . . .

It seems that prior to EDT 110, she avoided her university library, whereas now, she feels confident enough to use the physical space and the library's website.

Another student added:

Instead of using Google Scholar, I now rely more on the library portal, with journals to search for scholarly references and sources. Also, originally, I have strayed away from using books in research. Now, after completing this course, I have found books to be very useful for research in explaining broad topics and giving specific sources to look at for more specific information that pertain to my topic of interest. Lastly, after this course, I feel more comfortable with using the library for searches. After much practice in the course with the professors being librarians, I understand how to conduct meaningful searches and use the library for my advantage without feeling overwhelmed.

Yet another student agreed:

I was hoping by the end [of EDT 110] to be more familiar with the library and how to better use its resources not only for research but in general. I am very pleased with the tools that we were able to learn about while in this class. I now know many more ways to try to seek out the information I need. Also, I know how to differentiate between credible sources and non-credible sources of information as well. I learned that research is tricky if you don't know how to go about finding information and if you don't pay attention to where the information is coming from...

In addition to experiencing increased confidence and comfort with using the library, students also practice IL skills that ultimately help them develop skills to be better lifelong learners.

Information Literacy Competency Engagement

During reflection assignments and activities, many students demonstrate that they acquire specific performance outcomes outlined in the Association of College and Research Libraries (ACRL) Information Literacy Competency Standards. In this section, I will incorporate student reactions—written and verbal—as proof of engagement with some specific IL skills.

Standard one states, "The information literate student determines the nature and extent of the information needed" (ACRL 2000). Students indicate that they see value in helping solve community problems through conducting research on behalf of the community partner. In a sense, this affirms that they feel the information need they are addressing is a worthy activity. One student wrote, "The research is very helpful to Project READ because they only have one full-time [staff] member... [and] they do not have much time to spend researching. I feel because of my help in the research, I am helping Dayton become more literate." Although the instructors and the community partner negotiate and define the research question, students share responsibility for deciding what kinds of sources would be appropriate and how much information is sufficient to answer the question.

A few students named specific skills acquired during the course, such as effective keyword searching. One demonstrated that she learned that professionals often have a different vocabulary when she said it is important to try multiple searches with different keywords to "avoid missing critical information." At least two of her classmates agreed that an important skill they acquired during this class was effective keyword searching. These outcomes relate to IL competency standard two: "The information literate student accesses needed information effectively and efficiently" (ACRL 2000).

Some students supply evidence that they develop performance outcomes tied to standard number three: "The information literate student evaluates information and its sources critically and incorporates selected information into his or her knowledge base and value system" (ACRL 2000). One stated: "[Before this class,] I was always the kind of person who would not really research. I would find the first thing and click on it and say I was finished." Another student shared similar thoughts: "I used to think I could find everything I needed, but I realize now that I was only skimming the surface." She continued: "This course has helped me to become more involved with using all the resources that the library has to offer. I originally only used the Internet and did not use the books or librarians for help. This class required me to use both, which I appreciate." One of their classmates described a similar experience: "Along the way, I struggled with finding some appropriate sources, but the feedback I received [from the instructors] helped me to overcome that hurdle and find more suitable references." Yet another student said she appreciated learning how to write annotations because they helped her "learn how to summarize important points in a resource."

IL standard four states: "The information literate student, individually or as a member of a group, uses information effectively to accomplish a specific purpose" (ACRL 2000). Instructors designed this course such that students tie their research skills to a meaningful purpose as they help solve a community problem. EDT 110 students understand that their work fills a specific purpose, unlike writing a paper that no one but the instructor reads. One student articulated this when he said: "Seeing everything come together in the end . . . it convinced me that our work was worthwhile; it wasn't just busy work."

Another emerging theme that comes out of reflection activities is students' awareness of the information landscape beyond websites and search engines. Nearly all reflections included an appreciation for reliable library resources and demonstrated a basic understanding of the invisible web. This awareness ties very closely to IL competency standard five, which states that the information literate student "understands many of the economic, legal, and social issues surrounding the use of information and accesses and uses information ethically and legally" (ACRL 2000). Other students supplied proof that they acquired skills related to standard five with such statements as: "I can use my new knowledge of the invisible web to find scholarly information from databases" and "I now know the difference between a scholarly journal article as opposed to a magazine article." Yet another student wrote: "I have always been good at researching topics on the World Wide Web. I have learned two major research skills in this class. I have never used the advanced search for Google or any other search engine; furthermore, I had no idea that there was an invisible web. This will help me get to the meat and potatoes of my personal research and academic research for upcoming classes." In addition, at least three student reflection papers mentioned increased comfort with citing sources. One student claimed in his reflection that he dropped a course the previous quarter due to a "crippling fear of annotated bibliographies." He said that he appreciated the time and effort we took to explain annotations and formatting citations.

Based on published literature about the outcomes of service-learning experiences and contemplations shared in student writings and group discussion, instructors feel confident that the service-learning IL course model has a significant impact on student learning and engagement, along with the potential to impact lifelong learning. Just as Kuh defined service learning as a high-impact practice (2008), Pascarella and Terenzini note that "although the evidence is sometimes mixed, service-learning courses appear to promote students' commitments to social justice, social activism, and changing social and political structures as well as to a sense of social responsibility and civic engagement" (2005, 611).

CONCLUSION

Throughout EDT 110, instructors observe substantial student engagement with library resources and IL competencies. Students supply examples as they reflect on their service-learning experience, as has been demonstrated throughout this chapter.

One student approached the instructors after the last class to tell them: "I loved this class!" While this level of demonstrative enthusiasm is rare, gratitude for the course content is fairly widespread. For example, three weeks after the winter quarter 2011 course ended, the instructors saw a former EDT 110 student in the library, who told them: "What I learned in your class really paid off. I know now where to go for research." Then, she echoed the comments of a number of students who came before her when she said: "I probably should have taken the class two years ago." She retained her newly acquired skills, and she has been able to apply them to her coursework this quarter. She also realized that she could have benefitted from these skills earlier in her college career. Not only did she gain skills and engage with library resources, but she also helped analyze and solve a community problem.

ACKNOWLEDGMENTS

I would like to thank my coteacher, Cheryl Lauricella, and our community partners: Children's Hunger Alliance and Project READ. I also need to acknowledge my supervisor, Sue Polanka, head of reference and instruction at Wright State University Libraries, and Sheila Shellabarger, associate university librarian for public services at Wright State University Libraries; Cathy Sayer, director of service learning at WSU; and Dr. Sarah Twill, WSU assistant professor of social work. EDT 110 would not be possible without their support.

REFERENCES

ACRL. "Information Literacy Competencies for Higher Education," 2000. http://www.ala.org/ala/mgrps/divs/acrl/standards/informationliteracycompetency.cfm.

Axelson, Rick D., and Arend Flick. "Defining Student Engagement." *Change: The Magazine of Higher Learning* 43, no. 1 (2011): 38–43. doi: 10.1080/00091383.2011.533096.

Barry, Maureen. "Research for the Greater Good: Incorporating Service-Learning in a For-Credit Information Literacy Course at Wright State University."*C&RL News* 22, no. 6 (2011): 345–348. http://crln.acrl.org/content/72/6/345.full.pdf.

Bringle, Robert G., and Julie A. Hatcher. "Reflection in Service Learning: Making Meaning of Experience." *Educational Horizons* 77, no. 4 (1999): 179–185.

Burns, Lenard T. "Make Sure It's Service Learning, Not Just Community Service." *Education Digest* 64, no. 2 (1998): 38–41.

Campus Compact. "Annual Membership Survey Results 2010," 2010. http://www.compact.org.

Eyler, Janet. "Reflection: Linking Service and Learning—Linking Students and Communities." *Journal of Social Issues* 58, no. 3 (2002): 517–534.

Eyler, Janet, and Dwight Giles. *Where's the Learning in Service-Learning?* San Francisco: Jossey-Bass, 1999.

Graham, Leah, and Panagiotis Takis Metaxas. "Of Course It's True, I Saw It on the Internet!: Critical Thinking in the Internet Era." *Communications of the ACM* 46, no. 5 (2003): 70–75.

Hernandez, Marcia, and Lorrie A. Knight. "Reinventing the Box: Faculty-Librarian Collaborative Efforts to Foster Service Learning for Political Engagement." *Journal for Civic Commitment* 14, no. 1 (2010): 1–15. http://www.mesacc.edu/other/engagement/Journal/Issue14/Hernandez.pdf.

Herther, Nancy K. "Service Learning and Engagement in the Academic Library: Operating Out of the Box." *C&RL News* 69, no. 7 (2008): 386–389. http://crln.acrl.org/content/69/7/386.full.pdf.

Honnet, Ellen P., and Susan J. Poulsen. "Principles of Good Practice in Combining Service and Learning: A Wingspread Special Report." Racine, WI: Johnson Foundation, 1989. Reprinted by the National Service-Learning Cooperative Clearinghouse. http://servicelearning.org/filemanager/download/Principles_of_Good_Practice_for_Combining_Service_and_Learning.pdf.

Kuh, George D., and Carol Geary Schneider. *High-Impact Educational Practices: What They Are, Who Has Access to Them, and Why They Matter.* Washington, DC: Association of American Colleges and Universities, 2008.

Nutefall, Jennifer E. "The Relationship Between Service Learning and Research." *Public Services Quarterly* 5, no. 4 (2009): 250–261.

Michaelsen, Larry K., Arletta Bauman Knight, and L. Dee Fink. *Team-based Learning: A Transformative Use of Small Groups in College Teaching.* Sterling, VA: Stylus Pub, 2004.

Pascarella, Ernest T., and Patrick T. Terenzini. *How College Affects Students: A Third Decade of Research.* San Francisco: Jossey-Bass, 2005.

Riddle, John S. "Where's the Library in Service Learning?: Models for Engaged Library Instruction." *Journal of Academic Librarianship* 29, no. 2 (2003): 71–81.

10

Developing a Marketing Plan for the Library by and for Students

Gary W. White, Head of Reference Collections and Research,
Penn State University Libraries

> "In the past 10 years there have been tremendous changes in society that affect the entire concept of what a library is and does. Libraries are under threat. They face critical issues that threaten their very existence.... They face increased competition and the impact of new technologies. But these threats may also be challenges. They give libraries the opportunity to redesign their own future."

Several colleagues were asked to read this quote and to provide feedback on whether they thought this statement describes the current environment for libraries. Uniformly, they agreed. They were then informed that this quote was taken from an article written more than 15 years ago (Denham 1995, cited by Dodsworth 1998).

Strategic planning is not new to librarians nor is the idea of marketing library services and collections. However, several significant changes have altered how librarians approach the process of strategic planning, specifically the trend to develop written marketing plans. During the past decade, there has been a greater emphasis on "libraries as place," with the design of collaborative spaces that are conducive to learning and which also include aesthetic and comfort features. The explosive growth of social media has the potential to use these channels as ways to market and promote the library. At the same time, fiscal constraints are driving librarians to place a greater emphasis on assessment, accountability, and outcomes, which have led librarians to develop measures to demonstrate student use and their impact on student learning.

Gaining a better understanding of how students perceive and use the library is driving much of the strategic planning and marketing planning in academic libraries. Librarians in recent years have placed a greater emphasis on marketing and a much greater commitment to becoming more user-centered organizations (Matthews 2009; Germano 2010). A common practice to garner student input is by conducting ad-hoc student focus groups (see Armstrong 2010; Becher and Flug 2006; Burhanna,

Seeholzer, and Salem 2009; Seeholzer and Salem 2011). While the information gathered from these types of interactions is valuable to librarians, these interactions are limited in scope and often offer little opportunity for the students to become actively involved in the topic of discussion beyond providing opinions or suggestions. This chapter describes how the University Libraries at Penn State partnered with the Smeal College of Business's Marketing Department in order to gain more in-depth student engagement in the library's marketing planning process and how this partnership has led to a greater organization-wide emphasis on marketing and further student engagement. This was done first through collaborating with marketing students in the MBA program and through the subsequent hiring of undergraduate marketing interns to work with the Libraries' marketing steering team.

BACKGROUND

In 2004, the Penn State University Libraries system was one of 202 library systems that participated in the LibQUAL+ survey project sponsored by the Association of Research Libraries and Texas A&M University and used the survey as an evaluation tool. While the survey found that library users were generally satisfied or very satisfied with library services and resources, it did show that users tended to use nonlibrary gateways, such as Google, and that service quality and physical library spaces are important.

In addition to LibQUAL+, two national studies provided further information about the use and perceptions of academic libraries. The first was the 2003 OCLC Environmental Scan: Pattern Recognition (OCLC Online Computer Library Center 2003) and the second was Perception of Libraries and Information Resources: A Report to the OCLC Membership (OCLC Online Computer Library Center 2005). These national surveys found that less than half of students use their libraries daily or weekly, that students tend to use a web search engine to start their research, and that library websites and databases are not used at all by many students.

At this time, there was also much discussion in the profession regarding methods to transform library spaces and services to meet the changing needs and demands of students. Many librarians were redesigning spaces and offering new programs and services, including learning commons, enhanced technologies, and a greater emphasis on instruction. Academic librarians were seeking ways to further integrate their services and collections into the intellectual and social fabric of colleges and universities.

MBA PROGRAM PARTNERSHIP

Armed with these trends and the desire to investigate local student use of the library and its resources and because of my role as a liaison to the Smeal College of Business at Penn State, we decided to approach the marketing department with the idea of using the University Libraries as a case study for their marketing classes. In fall 2005, a meeting was held with the coordinator of the marketing track in the Master of Business Administration (MBA) program and subsequently with several faculty members who taught courses in the program. They were presented with a proposal to use the Libraries as a case study for their classes by emphasizing the following reasons why it would be beneficial to students:

- The library is a service organization. Because service companies/organizations are more prevalent in today's economy, this would provide experience for students in addition to the more common manufacturing case studies that they use.

- Libraries are not-for-profit organizations, so measuring impact and success is much more difficult because we do not generally use financial/profitability measures. This would provide students with an opportunity to learn about assessment by using measures other than financial measures.
- Libraries have a wide and varied consumer/user base. While most of our users are generally from the traditional college-age user groups, reasons for visiting and using the library vary quite extensively. Libraries also serve undergraduates, graduate students, and faculty—all of whom use the library differently; they also serve many different user segments: international students, student athletes, first-year students, residents/dorm students, and distance education users, among others. How does a library best market its resources and services to a diverse clientele?
- The library would provide the students with a chance to study a real organization rather than a historical case study or theoretical case. Their recommendations might also be implemented, providing an opportunity for students to become more actively engaged in a project that would have real impact.

It was important to convey to the program planners what the students would learn from this project and how it would help them in their future careers.

However, another reason to interest the MBA marketing students was that it would benefit the Libraries. It would be difficult to develop a marketing study/plan alone because they are difficult and potentially expensive. The marketing MBA students at Penn State typically come into the program with at least two years of corporate marketing experience, so this project would provide the Libraries with valuable market research data that would have otherwise had to be commissioned. Among this class were students who came from corporate marketing jobs at several Fortune 500 companies, including Google and Microsoft. In addition, these students were also users of the Libraries, so they could use their experiences as customers/patrons to help inform the librarians through direct feedback from students. A side benefit is that the project created an opportunity for librarians and teaching faculty to work collaboratively on a student project that would benefit all who were involved.

The MBA marketing track coordinator and several faculty agreed that the Libraries would be a useful, real-life case study, and it was decided to integrate this case into two of the last-semester courses for second-year marketing MBA students: Brand Management (Marketing 532) and Marketing Strategy (Marketing 571). At that time, MBA courses were offered in concentrated, one-half-semester (seven-week) sessions, with the Brand Management course being held the first half of the Spring 2005 semester and the Marketing Strategy course the second half. These two classes consisted of the same group of 40 second-year MBA students, concentrating in marketing, who were using the library as their project in these two capstone courses.

Students in the Brand Management course were divided into seven teams. Each team was responsible for conducting an ethnographic study of library users and to conduct a brand audit of perceptions of the Libraries among users. Ethnographic research is a social science research methodology that grew out of anthropological research and generally refers to an array of techniques used to study humans in their environments, including observation, interviews, and surveys and questionnaires (Denzin and Lincoln 1998).

Ultimately, students in this course collected data from more than 1,000 users of the Libraries through interviews and surveys. Each team also met with library administrators to ask questions and to gather information about the Libraries. Teams also had access to strategic planning documents and other information items, including news items and other promotional activities about events in the library. Each team used this data to perform a SWOT (strengths, weaknesses, opportunities, and threats) analysis of the Libraries and to gather characteristics of the target audience (students). The SWOT analyses were then used for further work in the next course: Marketing Strategy.

Students in the Marketing Strategy course were again divided up into teams. In this course, teams were responsible for developing a formal marketing plan for the libraries, incorporating their findings from the ethnographic studies and SWOT analyses of the Brand Management course. This course was structured as a contest, with library administrators serving as judges for the formal presentations, which took place during the last week of the semester. The librarians donated cash prizes to the top teams and purchased books for the winners and for the runner-up teams, which were placed in the library along with a bookplate commemorating the class and their accomplishments.

Postcourse consultation with the faculty and students strongly show that the project was a win-win experience for the students and the library. Course faculty conveyed that the library as a case study was a challenging project and a valuable learning experience. Students felt the same way, as indicated by the winning team's feedback in a thank-you card sent after the course: "Thank you for the opportunity. The exercise was enlightening for us, and it was a more useful exercise to have a real client! Thank you for all of your time and consideration of our insights."

The courses also had another benefit of continuing the interest and engagement after the students graduated. For more than a year after the course, students would periodically visit or e-mail, asking about the Libraries and how their suggestions were being implemented. From the Libraries' perspective, not one but seven ready-made marketing plans were available that could be immediately started. Overall, the library administration feels that this was one of the best examples of student integration into the library, and it continues to bring benefits to the library through continued efforts to build on the results of the project.

MARKETING STEERING TEAM AND STUDENT ENGAGEMENT

The MBA student project served to energize the entire library staff and brought interest in marketing to all levels and departments within the library. A direct result of this project was the decision the following year (starting in 2006) to create a standing Marketing Steering Team group. With my academic background in marketing, I initiated the MBA project, recommended the formation of this group, and became its chair. Part of the charge was to continue the work on marketing planning and to develop a formal library-initiated plan that was aligned with the overall strategic plan and would contain a proposed budget for marketing-related expenses.

Because of the success in engaging students with the MBA project, the new marketing team decided early on to hire a marketing student intern to assist in its efforts. Using funding from a library endowment for this purpose, the team worked closely with the Marketing Department to advertise and select its first undergraduate student intern. The student hired was a senior majoring in marketing and advertising, and she served for the year as a consultant to the team and also worked closely with the group in the development of the library's first marketing communications and outreach plan, which would be aimed at the undergraduate student population. Specific responsibilities during the year were to research and benchmark marketing activities at other large research universities and to conduct peer focus groups for all undergraduate students at each academic year.

The experiences in having an active student intern as part of the initial marketing team were mutually beneficial to the student and to the Libraries. For the Libraries, having the student work to gain valuable information directly from her peers and to use her knowledge and prior experience in marketing to assist in the development of the Libraries' marketing plan and other marketing efforts was extremely helpful. The resulting first marketing plan, entitled *Marketing Communications and Outreach Plan 2007/2008* (Pennsylvania State University Libraries, 2007), focused on marketing efforts aimed at undergraduate students. The marketing plan outlined the following overall strategies:

- Creation of a general visual identity or logo and message or tag line
- Creation of an Open House welcome kit
- Development of a print advertisement campaign
- Modification of the "Guide to the Libraries" brochure
- Preparation of new color brochures for specific subject areas
- Use of screen savers and mouse pads for display of marketing messages
- Acquisition of coffee mugs and other giveaways
- Developing activities to emphasize "Library as Place"
- Improvement of process for sending out press releases about the libraries
- Preparation of an internal campaign to garner staff support of marketing and broad participation in marketing efforts
- Creation of a web-based Marketing Toolkit to offer helpful suggestions, resources, and examples of marketing efforts in place throughout the libraries

In addition to the formal, written marketing plan, the intern also assisted in the development of a web-based Marketing Toolkit, which was designed to provide resources to individuals within the libraries to assist with marketing efforts (Pennsylvania State University Libraries, 2011). The student intern found the experience valuable, as evidenced in a report submitted at the end of the year:

My role as consultant allowed me to demonstrate my knowledge of marketing and offer advice in an area in which [the library] was unfamiliar. It made me realize just how much marketing and advertising knowledge I have gained from my education experience, and see its direct application in a non-profit business segment that has a unique offering of services as much as products. Because of this internship, I was given the opportunity to work with adults and given that I am graduating this semester and heading into the 'real world' of adults, I gained a lot from this interaction. Furthermore, I was working to benefit a real business as opposed to a hypothetical classroom assignment. I felt like I had a lot to offer the committee with my education background and personal experiences, which made me feel like a valuable contributor. More importantly, I gained a working knowledge of independently designing a marketing strategy that will actually be implemented. I will be able to take this learning experience with me into the professional world and affect other businesses too. Thank you for this non-traditional educational opportunity. I feel privileged to have been able to serve in this role.

UNDERGRADUATE MARKETING INTERNS

After the success of the library's first marketing intern, the marketing teams have subsequently hired several marketing majors to serve as interns. Hiring of the interns is done by collaborating with the Marketing Department in the College of Business. Once the internship position is approved by library administration, typically by March of each spring semester, the marketing team works with the Marketing Department on campus to advertise and recruit an intern for the following academic year. The quality of the applicant pools has been very high, consisting of students with very high grade point averages and many who are leaders of academic organizations. Applicants are screened and interviewed during April, with a final decision before the end of spring semester.

For the next two years, the marketing team assigned background reading and other materials to interns over the summer so they will arrive on campus in the fall semester ready to begin their work. These materials include the broad library strategic plan and the past marketing plans. New interns are also asked to familiarize themselves with the library's organizational structure.

The focuses of the marketing team were on the use of social media as a marketing channel, on improved signage/way finding tools in the libraries, and on developing a marketing plan for the libraries' new knowledge/learning commons. During 2008–2009, the marketing intern was integrally involved in the formation of the University Libraries' second marketing and communications outreach plan which focused on meeting certain segments of the user population, including international students, distance-education students, dorm residents, and graduate students (Pennsylvania State University Libraries 2009).

Engaging student interns proved to be a win-win situation, especially in efforts to reach students via social media. As active users of various social media, the interns have proven invaluable in helping the Libraries to use these same channels in order to connect in meaningful ways with students. Students are also more receptive to messages from their peers, and having interns conduct student focus groups in order to gather information to inform our marketing decisions was very successful. The interns themselves continued to find these experiences beneficial for their future jobs and, as a side benefit, found them very useful for improving their own library research skills. At the conclusion of each student's internship, staff asked the interns to write a report about their experiences. The following are some direct quotes, which are being reprinted with permission from the students:

> The University Libraries marketing internship provided me with an opportunity to gain experience in a number of marketing functions. I performed competitive analyses, market trend outlines, customer research, and other tasks as a member of the marketing steering team. The experience has provided me with an invaluable base set of skills that apply to marketing and other disciplines.
>
> A sizeable portion of my time working was spent performing market and competition study, gauging library trends and exploring possible marketing avenues. As emerging social media were a focus in the internship, I scoured dozens of comparable university libraries' web sites for ideas that could be adapted to PSU Libraries' marketing needs. I also performed basic research of popular and emerging social media trends in order to determine which entities could act as touch points between the Libraries and its customers (students, faculty, alumni). Another initiative

examined the social media currently in use by librarians, with the hope that these largely individual efforts could be connected and supported with best practice guidelines.

I gained valuable experience in market research techniques through the process of focus group research. I was included in the planning stage of the process, deciding what questions were pertinent to the libraries' goals as well as how they would be presented to the group. I was given the lead on holding the focus group and summarizing the data as well. Finally, I was responsible for developing a marketing copy of the data for internal and external libraries use.

I would like to thank the libraries staff for allowing me to assist in the ongoing effort to provide exemplary service to students, faculty, and alumni. The work I have done to support the market steering team's initiatives has provided me with valuable work experience.

—Marketing Intern, 2009–2010

Most of my work revolved around consumer research (i.e., focus groups with students), environment scanning (exploring social media best practices), and initiating contact between the team and cooperating organizations (like the Undergraduate Association). In what I found to be an interesting dichotomy, my marketing coursework translated smoothly into my activities with the steering team, while my reluctance to go to the libraries and *DO* my marketing coursework helped me relate to the demands and mindset of the team's target audience. This experience prepared me to think like a consumer and a producer at the same time and see the relationship between the two more holistically, which is a critical skill in the work I do now.

—Marketing Intern, 2009–2010

This internship has helped me in my course work as well as my professional experience. The drafting of the KC [Knowledge Commons] Marketing Plan gave me prior experience that was directly related to a project in my global marketing class. The work I have been doing has given me desirable experience in the field of marketing that will help me in my career search.

—Marketing Intern, 2010–2011

Being a marketing major, I am always looking for ways to utilize the knowledge I have gained in the classroom in real life applications. Working on the marketing plan for the Knowledge Commons at University Park gave me this opportunity. It allowed me to apply concepts such as identifying a target market or competition as well as brainstorm creative ways to market the Knowledge Commons. I believe my knowledge from the classroom and previous projects allowed me to bring some level of expertise to the table for this project, but I also gained valuable experience that I can take with me to future projects.

—Marketing Intern, 2010–2011

RECOMMENDATIONS AND SUMMARY

Engaging students in the work of the library can be a rewarding experience for all. However, it is important that students come into the experience with the understanding that they will be considered part of a team effort and are expected to live up to expectations to participate. Librarians and staff also need to allow students to fully engage in their internship project. Interns are interested in these projects as a way to learn and to gain experience, so they need to be given the freedom to take on projects and to manage them independently. For it to be meaningful, interns must be able to come away with experience and results that they can use to assist in their future job search and in their future positions. To get these kinds of projects going, it is vital to work with academic departments and to gain buy-in from the academic leadership.

The project involving MBA students described in this chapter demonstrates the value that a collaborative effort can bring to students and the library. Working with academic administrators to plan the project will help ensure a valuable learning experience for students that will also result in satisfying and tangible outcomes for the library.

In the academic library setting, student interns are a great way to get feedback from students and to help staff communicate with students in meaningful and useful ways. For example, interns conducted peer focus groups, and results show that students seem to be much more open about their opinions when speaking to a peer. Interns have also thought of innovative uses of social media that librarians and library staff probably would not have. Another benefit is that working with interns serves to change stereotypes of libraries and librarians!

In summary, student engagement through internships and student projects has led to successful collaborations for a library's marketing efforts. The key points to remember are to work closely with academic administrators to plan the project; demonstrate the value of the proposed project to outside administrators and faculty, with an emphasis on how the project or internship will benefit students; actively engage the students in the work and allow them latitude to shape the scope of their learning experiences; and provide them with some tangible results and work experiences that they can use in their future endeavors.

REFERENCES

Armstrong, Alison. "Utilizing Undergraduate Student Focus Groups to Navigate Difficult Budget Times." *Library Leadership & Management* 24, no. 3 (2010): 82–87.

Becher, Melissa L., and Janice L. Flug. "Using Student Focus Groups to Inform Library Planning and Marketing." *College & Undergraduate Libraries* 12, no. 1–2 (2006): 1–18.

Burhanna, Kenneth J., Jamie Seeholzer, and Joseph A. Salem. "No Natives Here: A Focus Group Study of Student Perceptions of Web 2.0 and the Academic Library." *The Journal of Academic Librarianship* 35, no. 6 (2009): 523–533.

Denham, Rudi. "Strategic Planning: Creating the Future." *Feliciter* 41 (1995): 38.

Denzin, Norman K., and Yvonna S. Lincoln. *The Landscape of Qualitative Research: Theories and Issues.* Thousand Oaks, CA: Sage, 1998.

Dodsworth, Ellen. "Marketing Academic Libraries: A Necessary Plan." *The Journal of Academic Librarianship* 24, no. 4 (1998): 320–322.

Germano, Michael A. "Narrative-Based Library Marketing: Selling Your Library's Value During Tough Economic Times." *The Bottom Line: Managing Library Finances* 23, no. 1 (2010): 5–17.

Matthews, Brian S. *Marketing Today's Academic Library: A Bold New Approach to Communicating with Students.* Chicago: American Library Association, 2009.

OCLC Online Computer Library Center. *The 2003 OCLC Environmental Scan: Pattern Recognition.* Dublin, OH: OCLC Online Computer Library Center, 2003. http://www.oclc.org/reports/escan/introduction/default.htm.

OCLC Online Computer Library Center. *Perception of Libraries and Information Resources: A Report to the OCLC Membership.* Dublin, OH: OCLC Online Computer Library Center, 2005. http://www.oclc.org/reports/pdfs/Percept_all.pdf.

Pennsylvania State University Libraries. *Marketing Toolkit*, 2011. http://www.libraries.psu.edu/psul/toolkits/marketingtoolkit.html.

Pennsylvania State University Libraries. *Marketing Steering Team Web Site*, 2009. http://www.libraries.psu.edu/psul/groups/marketingteam.html.

Pennsylvania State University Libraries. *Marketing Communications and Outreach Plan 2007/ 2008*, 2007. http://www.libraries.psu.edu/content/dam/psul/up/pram/documents/marketingplan.pdf.

Seeholzer, Jamie, and Joseph A. Salem. "Library on the Go: A Focus Group Study of the Mobile Web and the Academic Library." *College & Research Libraries* 72, no. 1 (2011): 9–20.

11

MInDSpace: New Media, Mashups, and Learning

Jacqueline M. Fritz, Instructor, Learning Technologies
Liaison, Bucks County Community College

INTRODUCTION

Academic libraries provide access to resources and services that engage students and ultimately empower students to succeed academically and professionally. To facilitate students' learning of essential skills for the workforce and academia, Bucks County Community College (Bucks) created a Media and Instructional Design Space (MInDSpace) in the Newtown, Pennsylvania, campus. The MInDSpace environment, created in 2009, includes physical and virtual (http://www.bucks.libguides.com/mindspace; http://www.bucks.edu/academics/learn/library/mindspace) resources and services.

In 2010, resources and services were expanded to the Lower Bucks County Community College campus, Upper Bucks County Community College campus, and the eLearning virtual Bucks County Community College campus. The MInDSpace team includes librarians, learning technologists, and an instructional designer. The team collaborates to provide the multitude of services required to support the creation and completion of projects that require students to use emerging technology and new media resources.

The student work conducted in MInDSpace involves the development of a set of skills that the MInDSpace team refers to as new media literacies (Jenkins 2009, 29–32). These skills include evaluating media, producing media, using emerging technologies, conducting research, creating citations, and understanding copyright and fair use. The MInDSpace team supports student engagement in the Bucks libraries by providing resources and services to develop new media literacy projects. In turn, the students develop collaboration skills, critical thinking abilities, and workforce 2020 skills, and they strengthen their visual, information, media, and technological literacy skills.

FOUNDING PRINCIPLES OF MINDSPACE

The Learning Resources administrators and faculty at Bucks developed the MInDSpace resources, services, and physical space after researching published learning theories, attending conferences, and visiting existing media commons and learning commons spaces. Gardner's theory of multiple intelligences provided the foundation for subsequent researchers to evaluate his theory that humans retain information and complete tasks through a variety of tactile, visual, and audio channels (Gardner 1993).

The literature on learning theory supports using combinations of tactile, visual, and auditory instructional tools to facilitate successful learning. This learning theory was implemented in practical classroom applications. Researchers studied the impact of using multimedia resources in the classroom and found that "multimedia instructional messages that are designed in light of how the human mind works are more likely to lead to meaningful learning than those that are not" (Mayer 2005, 32). As a result of learning theory research, elementary and secondary schools, colleges, and universities began supporting students and faculty in using new media resources and emerging technologies.

Bucks administrators and faculty attended several conference presentations that highlighted media, instructional design, and emerging technology concepts and services. A presentation by David Toccafondi and Anu Vedantham (NMC Summer Conference 2008) included demonstrating student video mashup projects and the achievements students made in learning the curricular objectives relevant to the project. The examples of student work demonstrated at the conference sparked an interest among the Bucks faculty and administrators in attendance and launched the conversation to determine how to implement services and provide resources to support the use of new media and emerging technologies in the Bucks curriculum. Additional conference presentations helped shape the direction and goals of MInDSpace.

Instructional design, media literacy, and learning technology leaders in higher education piloted, reviewed, and shared their experiences in developing and supporting new media and emerging technology assignments. The presentation by Peter Decherney, Renee Hobbs, Susan Simon, and Anu Vedantham (EDUCAUSE Annual Conference 2008) demonstrated the impact of successful assignment design on student learning and media literacy. The concepts introduced in learning theories were demonstrated through tangible examples of assignments and student work. The examples demonstrated at the conference presentation included video mashup assignments completed in place of traditional research papers in freshman writing seminar courses. Student and faculty feedback and assessment of the video mashup project supported the benefits of using new media instructional techniques.

Based on reports at the conference, observations of students completing these video mashup assignments revealed that students engage with the material and actually spend more time on the mashup video than they do on a traditional research paper. Instructional designers highlighted the importance of developing clear assignment objectives to generate excellent results from the students. Presenters noted that assessing video projects appropriately, making students aware of the assessment criteria, and educating students on copyright and fair use were essential components to new media projects. These conference presentations provided a great opportunity for other institutions like Bucks to get ideas and determine how to implement programs and new media services.

The learning theories—reinforced by assignments, examples of student work, and student and faculty feedback from other institutions—inspired Bucks administrators and faculty to create a space and provide services relating to implementing new media literacies in the curriculum. The Bucks group recognized the opportunity to support new media and emerging technology assignments in order to facilitate student success. About 70 percent of the students score in the developmental reading and writing level on their entrance exams (Yetman 2010). These students need to complete introductory reading comprehension and rhetoric courses before taking college-level composition courses. Completing a successful transition from developmental reading and writing courses to college-level composition courses requires students to quickly improve their skills.

The Bucks group assessing the need for new media and emerging technology resources and services identified that video mashups and new media projects require research, organization, identifying a main topic and supporting details, and citations. These traditional skills are completed in nontraditional means. Students need to use pictures, videos, images, audio files, text, and new media/emerging technology tools to compose the final product. The group decided that a space, resources, and services would need to be developed to best support students and faculty in completing the nontraditional and traditional components of a new media or emerging technology assignment.

After determining the relationship among learning theory, results from other institutions, and relevancy to Bucks students, the faculty and administrators began visiting information commons at other colleges and universities. After visiting other spaces, the group decided that in addition to providing a functional space, faculty and administrators wanted an area that provided more than just another computer lab. The space designated to the MInDSpace project is in the library. By building an active, innovative learning space in the library, the project became a representation of the future for progressive libraries.

Karl Carter, director of Learning Technologies, determined the layout of the space, furniture, and equipment to encourage creative thinking. "One limitation to designing the space was the physical requirements of power and networking, and this forced the computer table layout around the perimeter of the room. Placing chairs with wheels at the end of these tables helped to minimize the confining perimeter layout. The chair selection enables students and faculty working in the space to collaborate by grouping around sets of computer tables" (K. Carter, pers. comm.). This is important because many of the new media literacy projects being developed are group oriented in nature. Other design elements helped to facilitate collaboration and group discussion. Round tables in the center of the space provide ample room for groups of students. Also, the tables accommodate small classes visiting the space to learn how to use various learning technologies, such as iPods and handheld cameras.

Special events and professional development activities are also held in the space. A large HD screen with Internet connectivity is visible from the round tables, and this is used for presentations and webinars. "The layout of the space promotes efficient group work, use of technology, and collaboration" (K. Carter, pers. comm.).

The layout of the space is further enhanced by design elements. In addition to providing function, "the space was constructed to encourage creativity and to support student and faculty work" (K. Carter, pers. comm.). To create this environment, artwork from the arts department faculty was obtained and displayed throughout the space.

Student large-format photography adorns the walls of the space. To further emphasize the creative environment, a glassblowing artist and faculty member contributed 10 different glass lamps to place on the ends of each set of computer tables. "The photography, faculty art, and colorful glow of the blown-glass lamps significantly impact the look and feel of the space. These additions elevate the learning space above the 'computer lab' distinction. The redesigned space became a landmark on campus. It is not unusual to hear people identify the space by the glass lamps" (K. Carter, pers. comm.). This gave increased visibility to the library itself. MInDSpace is now known as the area "with the lamps," where students and faculty can come to work together on new media literacy projects.

In fall 2009, MInDSpace started providing access to new media resources and emerging technologies, including Macs and PCs, flatbed scanners, group workspace, and a variety of equipment, such as handheld cameras, microphones, etc. In the past two years, MInDSpace grew to include instructional design assistance, support to students and faculty in utilizing new media and emerging technology tools, new media literacy instruction, equipment rental, and videoconferencing or special event setup and support. Since implementing the MInDSpace services, faculty collaborated with the MInDSpace team to design assignments and use emerging technology tools. The skills acquired by the faculty are evident in the number of excellent well-designed assignments given to the students.

WORKING WITH FACULTY TO CREATE EFFECTIVE ASSIGNMENTS

Whether faculty members modify a pre-existing assignment or create a new assignment, the MInDSpace team provides services to aid faculty in the assignment design process. The MInDSpace librarians and instructional designer work with classroom faculty to apply "backward design" methods to assignment building (Wiggins and McTighe 2005). This is done to create new media project assignments that maximize student learning. These comprehensive assignments include clearly defined learning objectives and procedures for students to complete in order to fulfill those learning objectives.

The instructors also develop an assessment tool to evaluate how well students completed the procedures to meet the learning objectives. Including information on required media elements and instructions on using new media resources and emerging technology tools helps students understand the parameters of the project. MInDSpace team members work with faculty to write procedures to use new media resources and emerging technology tools. Writing an assignment to include traditional and nontraditional objectives, procedures, and assessment requires not only an understanding of the traditional outcomes but also an understanding of the technology tools needed to produce those outcomes. Faculty, MInDSpace librarians, and instructional designers collaborate to develop assignments through various professional development activities and one-on-one sessions.

Over the course of the academic year, several professional development events are offered to faculty, including scheduled meetings and roundtables, attendance at internal conference seminars and workshops, and an opportunity to apply to participate in a weeklong new media literacies institute.

The new media literacies institute affords faculty the experience of learning about new media literacies and multimodal learning pedagogies. After studying the theories, faculty members develop assignments that apply the theoretical knowledge to learning objectives for the courses they instruct. During the institute, faculty assume the role of a student by completing a group video mashup assignment. This activity provides faculty with the opportunity to critically analyze the objectives, procedures, and assessment criteria outlined in the assignment. Completing the assignment also requires faculty to use new technologies (such as movie-editing software) and unfamiliar resources (such as photos and videos).

One instructor built a digital poster by using web tools, video editing, and multimedia research to demonstrate the relationship between Polynesian culture and food choices. In class, students used the poster to facilitate discussion. Several faculty members in the language and literature department used video editing to represent the relationship between themes in the context of a novel and the context of everyday life. Combining those elements helped students learn the themes before writing and researching.

Another faculty member felt that "using media literacy helps move some of us who have been teaching for a long time into the current age. It encourages students whom we are teaching with the premise that if the 'old dog' is interested in learning 'new tricks' that they should also be interested in learning" (Marilyn Henry, pers. comm.).

After completing the video mashup assignment, faculty create an assignment that requires students to use new media resources and emerging technology tools. The faculty complete the assignment they created to identify weak components to their assignment. Faculty leave the institute with an assignment ready to implement in at least one of their courses or to pilot emerging technologies or new media resources as instructional tools.

Many faculty who complete the media literacies institute use video mashup assignments to build the same skills a student would need to compose a traditional research paper. The assignment requires the student to structure the video mashup to parallel that of a traditional research paper. Librarians or the instructional designer collaborate with faculty to translate traditional research paper requirements to requirements relevant to completing a video mashup. For example, students often create an outline and annotated bibliography or rough draft to submit before they complete their final research paper.

In completing a video mashup, faculty are advised to require students to submit an outline and a storyboard. These smaller assignments scaffold the overall research project to provide students with feedback. Like a research paper, the video mashup must support a thesis statement. The video must parallel research paper structure by introducing a topic, providing supporting details, and concluding the topic. References or works cited are required in the research paper and in the video mashup.

The medium of delivery is the main difference between the video mashup project and the research paper assignment. Completing this assignment requires students to use traditional scholarship skills, such as outlining, researching, analyzing, evaluating, citing, and organizing information to create a cohesive product. Designing an assignment to guide students through the process required to successfully complete a video mashup assignment presents some challenges that MInDSpace librarians and the instructional designer help faculty solve.

COLLABORATING WITH CLASSES

New media literacy projects assigned in any course may include instructional sessions that vary in content, scope, and objective to correspond to the nature of the course receiving new media literacy instruction. Librarians teach these instructional sessions, which focus on an assignment for a course that requires students to learn one or more new media literacy concepts: media produced for mass culture, media produced for popular culture, authoring media, and creating spreadable (social network) media (Jenkins 2011). This approach allows fluidity and the freedom for faculty to facilitate the acquisition of new media literacies as relevant to curriculum specific objectives.

Paul Proces, new media librarian, summarizes the theory supporting the Bucks approach to new media literacy: "The slate of new literacies of various types has its genesis in asking a fundamentally important question: 'Given the enormous changes wrought by information technology in society at large, shouldn't education re-examine the basic skills students need?' For media education at Bucks, the new fundamentals focus on four areas: media practice, media production, media literacy, and media studies. MInDSpace touches on all of these to some degree while acknowledging that in-depth media studies courses like film appreciation are done in another department: Communications Studies. The recognition of a fractured and distributed set of understandings and disciplinary 'takes' on media education is the starting point for successful collaboration" (P. Proces, pers. comm.).

With this approach, librarians collaborate with faculty specializing in a variety of disciplines during professional development activities. In three academic semesters, 75 faculty members collaborated with librarians or instructional designers to create assignments for their courses. The courses include effective speaking, composition, biology, computer science, women's studies, sociology, psychology, integration of knowledge (http://www.bucks.edu/catalog/intg.php), nursing, paralegal, American English as a second language (AESL), and world literature.

The variety of subject disciplines requiring the completion of new media literacy assignments creates many collaborative opportunities. The process involved in collaborating with a class in developing these new media literacy assignments involves the faculty teaching the course, the students in the course, and the entire MInDSpace team. The projects involve technology, research, citation, and instructional design.

The team uses each person's strengths and provides comprehensive service to the class of students and the faculty. The collaboration begins with the faculty following up on a professional development event, word of mouth from fellow faculty members, campus newsletters, or the promotional graphic postcard of the space and services. Then, the faculty and librarians analyze the assignment and recommend necessary adjustments. The assignment ultimately requires students to fulfill new media literacy objectives and course objectives.

Once the students receive the assignment, librarians instruct the students on how to access, analyze, evaluate, and communicate new media resources by using emerging technology tools. Depending on the schedule of the course, up to three sessions can be scheduled. After students receive instruction, they are encouraged to use the MInDSpace area of the library to complete their assignments. All classes receiving MInDSpace services or using the resources in the space impact the MInDSpace team because the team learns from the students just as the students learn from the team.

As students work through the assignment, they acquire new skills. They are often challenged by the technology, and the staff guides the students to find solutions to the technological mishaps. Working with students through the process of creating a new media project has given all MInDSpace users, staff, faculty, and students the opportunity to sharpen their skills, recognize the common issues in completing new media projects, and identify solutions to those problems.

In many classes, students embrace the challenges of the new media projects assigned to them and demonstrate an incredible growth in research, composition, critical thinking, and technology skills. The faculty members for these courses also embrace the challenge of creating a successful new media literacy assignment that requires students to demonstrate new media literacy skills, technology skills, and an understanding of the course objectives. Faculty who took the risk of trying new assignments gained experience in assignment design. Changing and adapting assignments to utilize new technologies and new media resources also challenged faculty to find a context for their subject discipline in today's increasingly digital and social resources.

An early adopter to the new instructional methods supported in MInDSpace, faculty member Max Probst of Sociology and Women's Studies recognized the benefits of assigning new media projects to his students:

> Students are bombarded by media images on a daily basis. Assignments that require students to create, analyze, and present media builds a classroom experience that teaches beyond blind consumption and gives space to evaluating the components represented in what we see and hear through media presentation. (M. Probst, pers. comm.)

The students in his women's studies course completed a video mashup assignment as their final project for the spring 2010 semester. The students met for several new media literacy sessions. In groups, they developed outlines, storyboards, and informal annotated bibliographies to organize the resources for their project. Many of the students had never used technology to the level required to complete a video mashup assignment nor had they conducted media research. Working through their troubleshooting research and technology questions helped the MInDSpace team to improve its instruction techniques and learning materials.

Another early adopter to MInDSpace services and resources used the emerging technology tools and support. An AESL faculty member piloted a language learning assignment with MInDSpace. This assignment required students to download tracks from the Bucks County Community College iTunes U account onto an iPod borrowed from MInDSpace. The faculty worked with the instructional designer to create the assignment and the iTunes U account. Students visited MInDSpace to receive their iPods and instructions on how to use them.

The students listened to idiom stories and pronunciation videos. The tracks and videos helped them complete an assignment in which they had to write a paragraph and record their reading of the paragraph. After the students completed the assignment, the faculty evaluated their experience to determine the usefulness in using the iPods. Students answered questions and wrote comments to summarize their experience in using the iPods. One student commented: "I would like to use this iPod for other courses because it really helps me in some of my pronunciations. It's just like I am watching a native speaker helping me to pronounce some word and I am saying it after him or her" (Linn Lisher, pers. comm.). The results of the survey demonstrated that students liked listening to and watching the content on a mobile platform. Because many students work, have families, and attend school, the iPod provided flexibility in reviewing course content. As students used the iPods, they could revisit MInDSpace to review their use or to troubleshoot any problems. This collaboration further developed the emerging technology resources and services.

As demonstrated by the previous examples, MInDSpace services are provided for new media and emerging technology-based assignments. Students can receive many of these services in online and face-to-face classroom environments. MInDSpace and the teaching team for the Integration of Knowledge (INTG) Metapatterns course collaborated to provide entirely online instruction and resources to the students in the course.

Bucks has an embedded librarian program (eBrarian) in place, started by the Online Learning and Information Literacy Librarians, to provide information literacy and new media literacy instruction to students in online courses (Hemmig and Montet 2010, 406). To provide the eBrarian services for the INTG course, two librarians used the web resource LibGuides (http://www.libguides.com) and worked together to build a collection of online tutorials and resources necessary for the students to work as a group to complete a video mashup assignment.

The tutorials included researching various media collections, researching databases, creating an outline for the video, creating a storyboard to organize the researched media and text in a structured narrative, and to use movie-editing software to create the video. Other resources provided to the students helped them create citations and contact librarians through chat widgets. All these resources were made available to students through a LibGuide. During the semester, students in the INTG course became familiar with using the guide to help them complete other assignments. One of the INTG Metapatterns faculty—the Online Learning Librarian—built the LibGuide specifically for the course. The MInDSpace librarians simply added a unique page to the pre-existing guide to provide information specific to the video mashup assignment (http://www.bucks.libguides.com/metapatterns).

In addition to the LibGuide, both librarians were embedded into the online course space. This allowed the librarians to answer students' questions through the discussion board space or via e-mail in the online course space. Making new media literacy resources available for one online course increased the scope of the MInDSpace services. The online tutorials and LibGuide pages are easily shared with other face-to-face and online courses, so this initial test run of online MInDSpace services helped to expand and improve services to students.

Collaborating with the early adopters of new media literacy and emerging technology assignments helped the MInDSpace team to further develop and improve services and course instruction. The collaboration among faculty and the MInDSpace team helped both groups learn and implement new techniques and pedagogies. The MInDSpace team tested, revised, and created new services with these courses. The growth of these services and instructional methods ultimately positively impacts the student's ability to learn new skills and traditional, subject-specific course objectives.

IMPACT OF MINDSPACE ON STUDENTS

The assignments students complete in MInDSpace require the use of nontraditional tactile, visual, and auditory skills as well as traditional research and composition skills.

As they develop their projects, students conduct research to find primary and secondary text, video, audio, and image resources. The students use technology tools and simple editing software or web applications to compose their project. Along the path of completing these assignments, students collaborate with librarians and MInDSpace staff. In utilizing library and MInDSpace resources to complete these projects, students learn new skills that are applicable not only to their classes but are also relevant to the expected demands of the future workplace.

Students receive new media literacy instruction from Bucks librarians. The structure of the instruction changes depending on the students' curricular needs. Students may need to use traditional media literacy skills to critically analyze the impact of popular news, advertising, television, and print media on a given subject. Other projects require students to treat new media resources, such as photos from online social photo galleries or quotes from blogs, as primary and secondary sources.

Each student completing a new media project learns how to access resources, analyze the composition of the resource, evaluate the relevance of the resource to the research topic or assignment requirements, and use the resource appropriately in a project. Completing new media literacy assignments further develops the students' ability to evaluate and use photo, video, and audio resources. All these skills require students to apply critical thinking to a world with which they are quite familiar: the world of Internet-based resources. Building the association between familiar resources and curriculum objectives ties the course subject matter to the student's day-to-day surroundings. The students experience their curriculum rather than just exposing themselves to it.

Students typically receive an assignment that requires the use of a web-based or simple movie-editing tool to organize and present various photos, videos, and text-based information. The students in Samantha Gross's American history course use a timeline generator tool to create timelines for specific periods in history. In course evaluations, the students anonymously indicated that the project was a great learning experience. "One student commented that this is material she will remember in years to come, but if she had been studying for a test, she would have memorized, and then not remembered the material" (S. Gross, pers. comm.). Integrating research with a visual and tactile task, such as compiling a visual, interactive timeline, helps students use a variety of skills, thus appealing to various learning styles. One student in Gross's class "remarked that after having discovered an image of Lincoln looking sad and exhausted during the Civil War, she really understood what Lincoln and the country had gone through in fighting this war" (S. Gross, pers. comm.). The student made the connection between emotional expression and physical appearance to the events occurring during the time the picture was taken. Utilizing a variety of resources helps students make those connections and deepen their understanding of the topic.

As students complete these new media literacy assignments, they explore collections of research material that range from blog and social networking sites to scholarly peer-reviewed resources. The librarians at Bucks work with students to find and evaluate appropriate resources in databases and online collections that offer access to Creative Commons licensed material.

Video mashup assignments and digital poster assignments often require students to demonstrate a first-person perspective on a current issue and to use factual information to support or refute the perspective. Students start their project by searching the web for blog posts, Facebook accounts, Twitter feeds, or web albums. These social media collections provide instant access to a first-person perspective.

To support the claims made in these first-person accounts, students search for secondary resources in the Bucks library collection. Students search for critical essays or scientific studies, and they use a variety of subscription resources, such as databases and electronic journals. To gather basic information, students use the online encyclopedias provided through the Bucks library database collection. For some topics, such as a paralegal assignment, students use the government documents housed in the library for quick facts relevant to their topic or thesis.

Along this path of fact finding, librarians help students identify keywords and find search strategies. Because tagging and user-generated titles classify most information on social media sites, librarians work with students to search for synonyms, slang, acronyms, or other nontraditional keywords to aid students in developing search strategies relevant to the nature of the collection.

During the Bucks Student Research Conference, one student noted that "completing the research for a video mashup was more difficult than a research paper because there are so many more resources to search for information" (Levine 2010). Students develop effective search strategies to navigate the overwhelming number of resources seemingly relevant to their project. As students find resources, they evaluate the content to determine bias or false information to choose resources that can be used appropriately and fairly in their project.

Librarians teach students to avoid heavily altered images—images manipulated to falsely portray a subject—and to avoid social media content not supported by research or other first-person perspectives. Also, they understand that copyright law protects works created by others. When looking at one resource, whether it is a picture, video, or article, students not only evaluate that resource to determine the legitimacy, accuracy, and relevance of the resource, but they also determine if they can use it fairly in their project. They learn these techniques in the new media literacy instruction sessions. Faculty members review the basics of copyright law and guidelines to help students determine fair use of resources. Also, the faculty guide students in developing the skills necessary to assess the quality of the resources in library and web-based collections.

Conducting research to include library resources and information from social networking sites and the other web-based resources improves the student's ability to critically analyze the information constantly presented in digital environments. In addition, because the students are becoming creators of their own content by completing this project, they become more aware of and invested in the true meaning of and reasons for copyright law and fair use of copyright materials.

In addition to students' developing academic skills while completing new media literacy assignments, students also develop skills essential to the workplace. Students build basic audio-, photo-, and video-editing skills. Students do not often realize the relevance of these skills to professional opportunities. When librarians and MInDSpace staff have the opportunity to discuss the project with the students, they encourage students to consider adding these skills to their résumés.

Students already in the workplace have a different perspective on using the technology and learning these new skills. As the librarians and MInDSpace staff aid these students, they sometimes share their plans for using their newly acquired movie-editing skills to create promotional videos for their employers. Those students already in the workplace are experiencing the shift in process and workflow undertaken by companies to meet the demands of an increasingly globalized workplace.

Many students also recognize the importance of working together as a group to complete these multiprocess new media literacy assignments. A student completed a survey anonymously and commented that "the mashup was both a fun and a very challenging assignment.... It was hard because we had to find ways to meet as a group and collaborate but we managed to put together a great project, and in the end, it was all worth it. It was a great team-building assignment and a great learning experience" (William Ford, pers. comm.). The collaborative nature of the assignments helps to prepare students for the change in the workplace to a collaborative, globalized environment.

This shift directly impacts our students and changes the skills they require to competitively perform in the workplace of tomorrow. "The workplace of tomorrow is being shaped today, driven primarily by globalization, the introduction of new ways of working, the usage of emerging technologies, and the shifting demographics of the workplace" (Meister and Willyerd 2010, 3). Students today need experience working in collaborative groups, conducting research, organizing information, and creating products through simple media-editing tools not only to build résumés for employment but to also improve their scholarship skills.

MASHUP CONTEST

The Bucks Mashup Contest (http://www.bucks.edu/mashup) is the common thread to the evolving space, services, and resources provided in MInDSpace. Before the space and services were provided, a group of Bucks faculty and administrators decided to hold a video mashup contest. The idea was to pilot a program to gauge students' and faculty interest in new media literacy projects. Once MInDSpace was created, the mashup contest served as a marketing tool to promote new media literacy assignments to the faculty. The number and quality of student entries to the mashup contest helped to serve as a measure, gauging the impact of MInDSpace resources and services on the project created by the student.

After attending the NMC and EDUCAUSE conference presentations that highlighted the positive impact of video mashup projects and contests at other institutions, such as Dartmouth and the University of Pennsylvania, Bucks County Community College faculty members in the Teaching and Learning with Technology Roundtable (TLTR) formed an action team to begin a campus-wide video mashup contest.

The faculty from liaison learning and teaching technologies, the director of the Lower Bucks Campus, and a business faculty member recognized that the mashup contest was a "gem of an idea" that would motivate faculty thinking about new media assignments as a curricular possibility (Marilyn Puchalski, pers. comm.). The mashup contest also began to get faculty to ask questions about video mashup projects.

The first mashup contest helped establish a dialogue among faculty about the benefits and drawbacks of using new media and emerging technology-based assignments. This first contest "raised community awareness of the idea to incorporate media to assignments" (M. Puchalski, pers. comm.). The MInDSpace team utilized the interest in new media literacy assignments sparked by the first mashup contest to promote the new services and resources being offered in the space.

The second annual mashup contest was held within the first year of MInDSpace implementation. Throughout the spring 2010 semester, librarians and learning technologists promoted the mashup contest through various professional development events. Faculty attended the events to learn the pedagogy supporting the use of new media literacy and emerging technology-based assignments. The mashup contest served as a platform on which faculty could pilot new media literacy assignments in their courses.

The INTG Self, Identity, and the Human Experience faculty first piloted the video mashup assignment. One faculty member reported that "the video mashup assignment is the perfect group assignment. For years, [we] struggled to find a group task that engages and teaches all the students in the team. The video mashup assignment serves this purpose well. The task is complex. It requires many different skill sets—from searching the Internet, evaluating appropriate source materials, visually imagining the assembly of those pieces, and the technical skill of working with the software tools to assemble the final project. When the project works, it engages most everyone on the team" (W. Ford, pers. comm.).

Students in these courses now had an additional incentive to complete a time-intensive, research-based video mashup assignment. They develop a complex set of skills, and they could win prizes sponsored by the Bucks Alumni Association in the video mashup contest.

The MInDSpace team and the Bucks Mashup team evaluated the differences between the first two contest entries. These differences demonstrated the impact of MInDSpace services and resources on the participation and submissions to the video mashup contest. The first contest had 7 submissions; the second had 24 submissions. In the first contest, a minority of the entries were videos completed for assignments, and in the second contest, 21 of the 24 entries were created for a course. Not only did the number of entries increase, but the quality of the videos also improved.

The executive director of the Lower Bucks campus (a mashup contest team cochair) evaluated the differences between submissions:

The quality of the assignments, the familiarity with the mash-up concept among faculty and students, and the quality of the submissions increased dramatically from year one to year two of the contest. This was due in large part to the service, assistance, and technical support provided by MInDSpace. Prior to the advent of MInDSpace, faculty did not have a place to go to receive guidance on how to create alternative multimedia assignments (like mash-ups), and students did not have a resource to help them work with multimedia software. This is what we learned when we implemented the first Bucks Global Video Mash-up contest. It really demonstrated the need for a teaching and learning resource, such as the MInDSpace concept. (Jim Sell, pers. comm.)

The assignment design resources now available to faculty through the implementation of MInDSpace also impacted the quality of the mashup contest entries.

Winning and notable student video mashups were created to follow the objectives and criteria of an assignment. The assignment design guides the student through building the structure of the video mashup. The students' research, organization, and composition skills also impact the overall quality of the video mashup. The mashup contest team of faculty and staff created a rubric to evaluate entries on their clarity/consistency, coherence, content/knowledge, creativity/originality, and citation. Using this rubric helped judges and the MInDSpace team to evaluate the strongest and weakest areas of students' understanding of the concepts taught to them in the new media literacy classes.

In both years of the contest, students consistently performed stronger in certain categories. The majority of the students did an excellent job researching, analyzing, and selecting appropriate content for their video mashups. The students also consistently produced creative, original work. The weakest areas of their mashups were the citation and coherence components. None of the mashups submitted in the first year of the contest received full points for those two categories. About one-fourth of the entries in the second year did not include citations or demonstrate a clear cohesive structure to their mashup, although all video mashup entries corresponding to an assignment designed in collaboration with MInDSpace received full marks for presenting a cohesive mashup.

After analyzing the differences between the two contests, MInDSpace librarians tweaked their new media literacy sessions to include online tutorials or face-to-face examples demonstrating the importance of organizing researched media and text and citing all media and text used in the project. The feedback and results from the mashup contest inform the services and instruction provided by the MInDSpace team, and the entries in the following year improved. This cycle of create, review, revise, change, and implement ensures that MInDSpace serves the needs of the students and faculty. In the future, the MInDSpace team plans on increasing the scope of the mashup contest and assessment strategies to further evaluate the impact of new media literacy projects on student learning.

CONCLUSION

In just two years, MInDSpace grew from a collaborative think tank idea to a program that impacts faculty and students on all four Bucks campuses. Professional development activities and the mashup contest inspired faculty to alter or create new assignments that require the use of emerging technologies and new media literacy skills. Faculty members work with librarians, instructional designers, and learning technologists to develop assignments and use new media resources and emerging technology tools in their classrooms.

MInDSpace projects promote library-student engagement. The students complete these assignments, and in doing so, they interact with librarians and learning technology staff to find resources and use media editing and creation tools. The students also receive focused instruction that strengthens their research, organization, critical thinking, and new media literacy skills. The students apply these skills to other courses at Bucks. The skills they learned by completing new media literacy assignments are also relevant to their future in academia and the workplace.

The mission of MInDSpace is to provide opportunities for students to become makers of meaning through the creation of multimedia productions. Engaging in such projects will lead to improved academic and professional success.

ACKNOWLEDGMENTS

I would like to acknowledge the contributions of Karl Carter, director of Learning Technologies, to the many discussions we have had about this chapter and about the design and vision for MInDSpace.

REFERENCES

Carter, Karl, Jacqueline M. Fritz, and Paul Proces. "MInDSpace." Bucks County Community College, 2012. http://www.bucks.edu/academics/learn/library/mindspace/.

Clossen, Amanda, Jacqueline Fritz, Paul Proces, and Matt Siebert. "MInDSpace Guide." Bucks County Community College LibGuides, 2011. http://www.bucks.libguides.com/mindspace.

Decherney, Peter, Renee Hobbs, Susan Simon, and Anu Vedantham. "Mashups, Remixes, and Video Culture: Engaging the YouTube Generation in the Classroom." Presentation at EDUCAUSE Annual Conference 2008, Orlando, FL, October 29, 2008.

Gardner, Howard. *Multiple Intelligences: The Theory in Practice*. New York: Basic Books, 1993.

Hemmig, William, and Margaret Montent. "The "Just for Me" Virtual Library: Enhancing an Embedded eBrarian Program." *Journal of Library Administration*, 50, no. 5 (2010): 657–669.

Jenkins, Henry. *Confronting the Challenges of Participatory Culture: Media Education for the 21st Century*. Cambridge, Massachusetts: MIT Press, 2009.

Jenkins, Henry. "From New Media Literacies to New Media Expertise: 'Confronting the Challenges of a Participatory Culture' Revisited." A Manifesto for Media Education, 2011. http://www.manifestoformediaeducation.co.uk/2011/01/henryjenkins.

Levin, Viktora. "Video Mashups on Teen Parents." Presentation at Department of Language and Literature Student Research Conference, Bucks County Community College, December 3, 2010.

Mayer, Richard E. *The Cambridge Handbook of Multimedia Learning*. New York: Cambridge University Press, 2005.

Meister, Jeanne C., and Kerri Willyerd. *The Workplace 2020: How Innovative Companies Attract, Develop, and Keep Tomorrow's Employees Today*. New York: HarperCollins Publishers, 2010.

National Association for Media Literacy Education. "The Basic Definition." *Media Literacy Defined*, 2011. http://namle.net/publications/media-literacy- definitions.

Toccafondi, David, and Anu Vedantham. "Five Minutes of Fame Award: Weigle Information Commons." Presentation at 2008 NMC Summer Conference, New Media Consortium, Princeton University, Princeton, NJ, June 13, 2008.

Wiggins, Grant P., and Jay McTighe. *Understanding by Design*. Alexandria, VA: Association for Supervision and Curriculum Development, 2005.

Yetman, Barbara. "Overview of 2010 Survey Results: The Community College Survey of Student Engagement (CCSSE)." Bucks County Community College, Institutional Research Department, August 23, 2010.

12

The Library as Studio: Enculturation, Student Engagement, and the Spaces of the Library

Patrick Tomlin, Art and Architecture Librarian, Virginia Tech

In what ways are library spaces designed to engage and encourage new modes of learning? Conversely, in what ways do such spaces affirm, lend authority to, or project dominant forms and ways of knowing? How are new technologies like laptops and mobile devices changing the way students learn within and interact with the library? How should they change our conception of library space? This chapter attends to these questions. It argues that focusing too closely on the ostensible separation of the physical and virtual spaces of the library runs the risk of losing sight of broader changes occurring in modes of student learning. These are changes that necessarily force a reconsideration of how the academic library confronts the task of student engagement.

THE ART AND ARCHITECTURE LIBRARY AT VIRGINIA TECH

This chapter also asks another question: What would it mean to call a library a studio? The design studio has long occupied a central place in architectural and visual arts education programs in the United States. Indeed, the intensity and involvement that characterizes the work of the studio is virtually unparalleled in other disciplines, excepting perhaps the sciences. The level of reflective activity undertaken within its setting requires and produces a diverse set of critical thinking skills (Dutton 1991; Snyder, Heckman, and Scialdone 2009). These characteristics point to the singularity of the studio as a pedagogical model, but they only begin to suggest how rich its potential might be for conceptualizing the work of the library. What would (re)conceiving the library as a studio entail for student engagement and outreach?

Such questions loom large at Virginia Tech's Art and Architecture Library, in part because the design studio itself is a vital presence in its daily activities. Located within the same building housing the School of Architecture and Design, library facilities are literally embedded in the teaching and learning activities of the university's College of

Architecture and Urban Studies. The library, which has only one entrance, is flanked by open architecture studios; as a result, one must first pass through the dynamic sights and sounds of the studio before entering it. Student desks are strewn with preliminary drawings and half-completed models. Studio walls are filled with arresting presentation posters and ideas in the process of being visualized. Perhaps professors lecture or circle around their classes, offering individual feedback. Students engage in collective dialogue or present their work in front of an audience of their peers or professionals for critique. This relationship between studio and library indelibly shapes the patron's experience of and response to the library as a physical space. Users are immersed in the muted but constant thrum of student activity going on just outside the library's doors.

If the boundary between studio and library is highly permeable, the plan of the Art and Architecture Library itself internalizes the essential pedagogical infrastructure of the studios around it, giving pride of place to a learning commons conducive to the specific nature of the work undertaken by architecture and design students and faculty. Within this space, library materials are only one aspect of a much broader spectrum of engagement with the processes of knowledge production within the disciplines the library serves. Before further clarifying the implications of its arrangement, a brief "tour" of the library is perhaps in order.

Transparency is a word used frequently when describing the Art and Architecture Library. Floor-to-ceiling glass windows line the entrance and exterior walls of the library, making its focal point—a large commons area with computers, modular tables and chairs—fully visible to those passing by within and outside the building. This element lends the space a distinct visual impact before users even enter it, offering a view of the library space and through to the grassy, tree-shaded campus beyond.

The unfolding spatial registers mean that the library serves as a sort of mediating zone—literally connecting the learning activities taking place within the School of Architecture with the larger university community. Library instruction sessions also take place in the learning commons area and are thus completely visible from within and outside the library. Because the circulation and reference desk close to the entrance is situated as an island, detached from library administrative offices behind it, the boundary between the workspaces of students and those of library staff is markedly porous. The resulting cumulative effect is, even at first glance, one of fluidity and transparency—a space often exuding a very studio-like air of "organized chaos."

Upon entering the library, one is immediately immersed in a space designed by architects for architecture students and in consultation with architecture faculty. Following a T-shaped plan, the commons area dominates the central axis of the plan and is surrounded on either side by a collection comprising approximately 90,000 volumes. Arranged to ideally accommodate multiple groups, the dozen reconfigurable tables and 10 computer stations making up the learning commons are highly attractive locations for students working on collaborative projects or undertaking group discussions. Of course, "nonlibrary" uses, ranging from meetings with faculty to general socializing, are also frequent. Pockets of individual seating scattered across various alcoves and nooks throughout the library invite more solitary forms of work, but it is this primary architectural space that attracts most users.

Punctuated with compelling objects, images, and colors, the library was carefully designed to function as a multifaceted learning object in itself. It contains a notable collection of furniture designed by canonical designers and architects of the twentieth century. These include original works by Mario Botta, Alvar Aalto, and Marcel Breuer as well as reproductions by Philippe Starck, Eileen Gray, and Aalto, among others. Original prints by Josef Albers and Robert Motherwell join a gallery of reproductions of works by other artists. Last but not least, the library's circulation desk, designed and built by a former Virginia Tech architecture faculty member, is a spectacular case study in the marriage of modern form and library-specific functionality. Combining strikingly diverse materials, including concrete, leather, rusticated steel, and three different varieties of wood, the sleek desk is often the object of class discussions, student analysis, and inevitable questions from first-time library users. Together, these objects immerse the viewer in an atmosphere of creativity and beauty and further draw the library—as a space where looking and touching go hand in hand with reading and writing—into the larger pedagogical mission of the College of Architecture and Urban Studies.

Moreover, the engagement activities of the Art and Architecture Library have been conceived within the context of the development of the Virginia Tech Libraries' College Librarian program. Launched in 1994, the program placed nearly half of the Libraries' nearly two-dozen reference librarians in offices located in the colleges of their subject specialization. As a "high tech, high touch" means for instilling and bringing visibility to library outreach, the College Librarian system provided subject expertise and opportunities for instruction and reference within close physical proximity to students and faculty.

Often described as "virtual branches," these offices attempted to harness in miniature form the branch's ability to focus a core set of tailored services, the development of close ties with faculty and students through close proximity to teaching and learning spaces, and one-on-one interaction (Seamans and Metz 2002; Schillie, Young, and Ariew 2000). Because of its relative physical centrality to the schools it serves and its commitment to the unique academic and research needs of architecture and design students and faculty, the Art and Architecture Library is in many ways the programmatic embodiment of the University Libraries' particular brand of student engagement.

THE LIBRARY AS STUDIO

Incoming first-year university students have only a distant memory—and one that will, with each successive freshman class, only further fade—of a time in which the Internet did *not* have a place in the learning process. For the great majority of them, learning has always been shaped to some degree by the forms of participatory involvement, collaboration, and extensive mobility engendered by the web.

Similarly, social experience and individual, self-directed learning are, for them, intertwined to a degree that may seem paradoxical and counterintuitive to others belonging to an older generation. Indeed, John Seeley Brown has called attention to the need for a greater understanding of the new forms through which student learning now takes place; this entails a shift away from the traditional quantitative assessment of *what* is learned and toward *how* learning occurs. The challenges of the current digital paradigm to the existing educational system "require that we re-conceptualize parts of our educational system," he writes, "and at the same time find ways to reinforce learning outside of formal schooling." He continues:

Luckily, successful models of teaching and learning already exist that we could emulate and build on. In the architecture studio, for example, all work in progress is made public. As a consequence, every student can see what every other student is doing; every student witnesses the strategies that others use to develop their designs. And there is public critique, typically by the master and perhaps several outside practitioners. The students not only hear each other's critiques, but because they were in some sense peripheral participants in the evolution of each other's work, they also have a moderately nuanced understanding of the design choices and constraints that led to the final result.... Also consider how students in studios start to pick up skills from each other; how they witness the wide variety of approaches to a design problem; and how they start to appreciate and learn from the struggles, the missteps, and the successes of their peers. Think about how they start to practice the social and intellectual skills that enable them collectively to become a reflective practicum. They are, in short, becoming acculturated into the practice of architecture. (Brown 2006, 18–19)

For Brown, the importance of the studio as a pedagogical model rests in the complex ways in which it enables students to reflect upon the learning process and to collectively engage the communication structures of the discipline.

Put differently, the studio (re)produces the disciplinary ways of knowing it embodies: through the collaboration, critique, dialogue, and skill sharing inherent in its spaces, students acquire knowledge about the profession. They gain a body of practical techniques and skills, including sketching, model making, and so forth, and glean theoretical knowledge, but they are also learning what it is to *be* an architect.

As Brown states, "Rather than learning *about* something, they are learning to *be* something, a crucial distinction" (Brown 2006, 19). One might argue, *contra* Brown that students are learning simultaneously about the profession *and* how to belong to it. Studio-based learning is dynamic and often transparent—a lens for viewing the culture and practices of the discipline as they exist in that moment and within the specific context of the studio.

Ironically, studio art and architecture students are sometimes ambivalent about the role of the art library within their own development as practitioners. Traditional research skills might appear external to the seemingly autonomous environment in which studio inquiry takes place at least as that inquiry is often popularly conceived, whereby the student achieves creative breakthroughs via a process of manual training (how to create) and self-discovery, ideation, and reflexivity (what to create) within the material confines of the studio.

This model relies only tangentially on external artistic references or information resources, and these are often encountered haphazardly (i.e., without formal library instruction, as the circumstances of browsing dictate). Finding a common ground between the distinctive work carried out by studio students, their perceptions of the art library, and the actual aims of library engagement is a distinct challenge running throughout the literature on art librarianship (Bennett 2006).

It should be emphasized here that the positive implications of using the studio model are as a template for library engagement, not a suggestion that the academic library would begin participating in group critiques or pinups. Reconceiving the library as studio—as a space in which dynamic inquiry and applied knowledge is fostered and where enculturation into an ever-encroaching "information society" takes place—not only minimizes the increasingly problematic division between physical and virtual resources, but it necessitates that both are used in the service of what Brown calls "learning to be," entailing a much more complex and nuanced vision of the library's role within the university. Indeed, this model veers close to the argument made by

Shapiro and Hughes, more than a decade ago, for the reconceptualization of information literacy as a liberal art. "Information and computer literacy, in the conventional sense, are functionally valuable technical skills," the two authors write,

> But information literacy should in fact be conceived more broadly as a new liberal art that extends from knowing how to use computers and access information to critical reflection on the nature of information itself, its technical infrastructure, and its social, cultural, and even philosophical context and impact—as essential to the mental framework of the educated information-age citizen as the trivium of basic liberal arts (grammar, logic and rhetoric) was to the educated person in medieval society. (Schapiro and Hughes 1996)

Here, information literacy is presented as the ability to critically approach new technologies of information and their attendant cognitive skills as they arise. For Shapiro and Hughes, it is viewed not as a static skill set to be passively received or only as the development of a repository of knowledge or methods but as a standard for active, lifelong learning. Their compelling characterization of information literacy as a dynamic and ongoing process remains fertile ground for further exploration within academic librarianship as a whole.

ART LIBRARIES IN THE DIGITAL AGE

One of the implicit aspects of Brown's formulation of "learning to be" is the way it highlights the specificity of media in the learning process. It is the media, not the message, so to speak, that is crucial. This has obvious implications for the contemporary academic art library, which has long sought to maintain some semblance of a balance between its physical and virtual components.

Despite cyclical declarations of the impending ascendancy of the digital library issued from various corners over the past two and a half decades, it is increasingly apparent that the virtual and physical spaces of the library have grown only more intertwined rather than separate. Far from fading into the background of the university community, supplanted by collections and automated services existing solely in digital formats, the library's role *qua* learning commons has been reinvigorated by renewed scrutiny, fresh theorization, and new methods of assessment.

Indeed, the explosive growth of digital resources has called attention to the diverse ways in which the physical spaces of academic libraries are being used and, in many cases, reconfigured in forms ostensibly unconnected to the material collections they house yet ultimately bound to a similar notion of accessibility. Rather than viewing them as separate spheres, then, it is perhaps more fruitful to address the virtual and physical dimensions of the contemporary academic library as simply different aspects of an increasingly hybridized and transformative institutional organism. While each aspect may meet different and equally essential needs, both must be effectively integrated into the educational and research missions of the surrounding academic institution in order to function properly (Gerke and Maness 2010).

Nowhere is this complexity more apparent than in the case of the art and design library. Even a cursory scan of the general academic art library would reveal a campus resource that has made a fine art (no pun intended) of straddling the traditional and unconventional. During a time of accelerated consolidation of library units, the art library holds a uniquely multifaceted identity. The physical spaces of art libraries are by turns—and often all at once—an extension of the artist's studio, a public space for collaboration, a retreat for private contemplation, and a local gallery. But the art library is also the site of accelerated development in the areas of digital resources and electronic content delivery (Wallach 2010).

Much of the intricacy of the current state of the contemporary art library stems from the research and technological needs of the disciplines it serves. Unlike the sciences, where the proliferation of electronic full-text journals, e-books, and online reference sources has resulted in a significant decrease in the need for maintaining print counterparts in those areas, the arts remain deeply invested in print materials. There are practical reasons for this: for example, the currency of scholarship in art history, design, and architecture usually outlasts that of the sciences and other technical fields.

More than this, the special status of the image, the two-dimensional reproduction of the three-dimensional work of art, and the juxtaposition of text and illustration within the scholarly production of these disciplines has proven a formidable obstacle for the widespread adoption of digital formats. The current technological limitations of digital image reproduction in electronic books and journals—from poor color fidelity to low display resolution and large file sizes, not to mention the tightening grip of copyright and intellectual property law—has meant that a transition paralleling that of the sciences has occurred slowly and unevenly.

On the other hand, adoption of digital technologies and web-based platforms in the area of visual resources has been extremely rapid and nearly total. Digital image collections have made many analog visual resources components, particularly slide collections, largely obsolete in recent years (except perhaps as fodder for digitization). Teaching and classroom experience have been subtly but radically transformed in the process. Because visual resources curatorship sometimes falls within the domain of the art library, this must also be contended with.

It is critical to highlight just how distinctive art library users' needs are as a result of these disciplinary characteristics. Because student research in the art and design disciplines is often driven as much by finding appropriate images as by locating a needed text, the accessibility of the library's collection can play an essential role in the efficacy of the search process. Students and faculty regularly search through the entire holdings for an artist to locate a particular, if previously unknown work—one that meets the criteria of their own project.

The act of browsing, of course, necessitates physical access to the library (Alger 2010). Particularly in studio courses, faculty not only encourage open-ended browsing of monographs and journals, but browsing is virtually *required*—an essential mechanism for fostering inspiration and experimentation. The sight of studio classes descending unexpectedly upon the library *en masse*—sent by their professors to search through books and journals for images relevant to a lecture or arising spontaneously from a conversation—is not an uncommon occurrence in many academic art and design libraries. The central location of Virginia Tech's Art and Architecture Library makes it a critical resource to have close at hand in such instances and offers a unique extension of the studio's animated learning environment.

The architecture and design student's experience of the art library is typically individualized and very often idiosyncratic, necessitating personalized and multifaceted library services in kind. It is an experience that is currently difficult—if not at times impossible—to replicate within electronic databases and digital resources noticeably built around text-based information needs and search patterns. Nor are such information requirements always easy to tackle through typical library research strategies. For example, reproductions of architectural details can often be notoriously difficult to find because they are infrequently or unsystematically indexed in either electronic databases or print materials. That said, in most art history courses and in student life in general, expectations for systematic, anytime delivery of electronic content—whether through full-text article databases and online indexes or as print materials—are increasingly the norm.

This entails planning library spaces for access to the general Internet and specific web-based library resources through computers or, as is the case more and more, wireless capabilities accessible by laptop and mobile devices throughout the entire library. Moreover, the steady increase in programs devoted to digital arts ensures that student needs will not remain static. The identity of the contemporary library, then, is one of hybridity; the task of the art librarian is that of finding a common ground between the traditional and the unconventional.

THE STUDIO IN PRACTICE: MOBILIZING STUDENT ENGAGEMENT

Despite the significant changes in information practices initiated by digital content and its modes of delivery—a drastic alteration of the means and speed by which information may be organized, accessed, and exchanged as a result of the Internet—academic libraries themselves have changed remarkably little in their approach to student engagement. That is, the *conventions* of library engagement have been slow to respond to the fundamental significance of the rapidly proliferating modes of collaborative, customized, active learning offered by the congruence of the web and current technologies (Gibson 2006).

As many scholars have noted, these technologies collapse any sound distinction between doing and learning, interaction and reception, creation and knowledge, individual and community practice (see Shirky 2008; Davidson and Goldberg 2009). For many students, everyday learning is networked, social, and, very often, situated—thanks to such mobile devices as laptops and smartphones. Indeed, the sheer mobility and diversity of these tools of communication and learning raise crucial questions about the nature of our definition of information literacy, the cornerstone of library engagement.

To what degree is it dependent upon static forms of content and categories of delivery? If, as Elizabeth Daley, has argued, "the multimedia language of the screen has become the current vernacular," how does this change the way we frame information literacy in instruction and other engagement contexts (Daley 2003, 33)?

Like all art libraries, the Art and Architecture Library at Virginia Tech is intended to facilitate learning within the disciplines it serves. But it is also designed at its most ideal to facilitate work and learning in a *manner* that conforms to and, indeed, replicates the structure of enculturation that takes place in the studio environment that characterizes those disciplines. Its layout is ideal for collaborative, interconnected, and open work similar to the kind occurring in the studio.

These aspects make it an ideal environment for exploring "learning to be" forms of engagement within a library context. The challenge that lies ahead rests, to paraphrase Brown, in moving from "learning about" library resources and information literacy skills in general toward "learning to be" information literate creative professionals in a world defined by the centrality of digital technologies. How can we transfer the fundamental experiences of the studio into the library spaces and its services?

Mobile technology itself provides one answer. In September 2010, the Art and Architecture Library purchased 20 Apple iPads for circulation among faculty and students at Virginia Tech. From the beginning, the project was conceived as a library-based case study in the use of mobile devices to target the information needs of a specific audience—in this case, the faculty and students of the College of Architecture and Urban Studies (CAUS). The availability of the iPads was advertised largely by word of mouth within the college and as users passed through the library. This proved effective in limiting the case study largely to its intended audience, although it also necessarily limited the visibility of our early adoption of this much-publicized mobile device.

The iPad is arguably the most ubiquitous sign of the emerging culture of mobile technology. Existing somewhere between the portability of the smartphone and the computing power of the laptop, the tablet has pushed to the forefront of personal mobile media devices. Although its popularity has been enormous from the beginning, the sphere of higher education was also quick to seize upon the iPad for its multifaceted educational potential as an e-book reader, real-time data collection device, and presentation tool, among other uses.

Because of their multiple possibilities, the iPads were launched with the aim of exploring how mobile technology might be utilized to assist the diverse information needs of CAUS students and faculty in particular. In large part, the low cost and direct availability of apps—or downloadable software applications—made this possible. Currently, nearly three dozen apps are preinstalled on each iPad before checkout, ranging from discipline-specific resources (such as the digital sketching and CAD programs Sketchbook Pro and Rhino) to general productivity apps (such as Pages for word processing and Keynote, Apple's presentation application). Links to the libraries' mobile interface are also present. Users can download additional apps during the loan period and retain access to individual selections—whether paid or free—via their personal iTunes accounts. These purchases are retained by the user upon return of the device to the library, at which time all personal information and software downloads are erased from the machine by an automated restore process.

Despite its emphasis on mobilizing content, the iPad also holds significant potential to enhance *in situ* library experience and student engagement. For example, the tablets have been used at the Art and Architecture Library to enable "roaming" assignments throughout the stacks during instruction sessions, where students learn about the library's layout, the various subject classifications, and the Library of Congress Classification system. They facilitate reference encounters and "teachable moments" anywhere within the library—detached from the physical locus of a computer terminal or reference desk.

More importantly, the iPad has provided the opportunity to lead discussions among students about the relationship between the physical and virtual resources at their disposal—how both are intertwined and, indeed, simply two sides of the same institutional coin. Its physical effect is compellingly decentering: its touch screen interface makes information seeking *physical* in a manner that is unfamiliar and highly appealing to many architecture and design students, who are themselves deeply immersed in the physical processes and ways of knowing that sketching and fabricating three-dimensional objects provoke. More importantly, as a device that seems to give as much weight to the *production* of new media as to its consumption, the iPad provides a singular point of entry into conversations about the necessity of reflexive engagement with traditional sources and processes of information delivery as well as the possible alternatives to each.

More generally, our iPads project has energized the perception of the library as a provider of innovative information resources among the community of the College of Architecture and Urban Studies. Apart from their everyday use by students and faculty, the tablets have been incorporated into studio competitions, seminar presentations, and grant proposals. Figure 12.1 illustrates one such use. Approached by an industrial design professor and his third-year studio in the School of Architecture and Design, the library loaned 10 iPads for use in their course-long research project on senior living sponsored by a local architecture firm. As the partnership came to a close with the end of the semester, the collaborative project culminated in the presentation of their ideas at a regional design conference. The tablets were integrated into the students' individual presentation posters—where they enabled slide shows of concept sketches and provided a springboard for discussion of the evolution of their ideas with conference attendees. Similarly, many architecture students have used the iPads to supplement the models and drawings they have presented during the frequent studio pinups held throughout the building during the semester (see Figure 12.2).

The iPad generates opportunities for inquiry-based learning and the development of new learning contexts that exist outside of the library—in either the virtual or physical sense—yet remain intangibly connected to it as a provided service. By occasioning collaborative projects with faculty, the iPads have allowed the library to take part in larger conversations about the links between information (multimedia) literacy as it is typically defined and its manifestation in more specific disciplinary ways of knowing and information seeking.

Of course, technologies come and go; the number of students at Virginia Tech who have their own iPads has grown exponentially since the Art and Architecture Library first began circulating them. But that ubiquity is, in a way, precisely the point. What the iPad and the growing coterie of mobile devices like it stress—flexibility, portability, interactivity, collaboration, user experience, and, above all, ease of access—

Figure 12.1
The iPad used in design student poster competition.
(Photo Credit: Akshay Sharma)

Figure 12.2
The iPad used in architecture course display.
(Photograph taken by the author)

progressively blur the boundaries that have traditionally separated academic from non-academic information needs (Hahn 2008).

As John Traxler recently argued, the "mobile learning" created by new technology "is not about 'mobile' as previously understood or about 'learning' as previously understood, but part of a new mobile conception of society" (2009, 5). If libraries are to remain dynamic vehicles for student engagement, the spaces that define them and the services they offer must adapt to this social change and its concomitant shift in ways of learning. The spaces of the library—real and virtual—must not only acknowledge shifts in media and technology, but they must also support "information enculturation." That is the growth of a learning community skilled in thinking critically about what it means to be an information-literate citizen in the mobile digital age.

REFERENCES

Alger, Jeff. "The Value of Architecture and Design Branch Libraries: A Case Study." *Art Documentation* 29, no. 2 (2010): 48–52.

Bennett, Hannah. "Bringing the Studio into the Library: Addressing the Research Needs of Studio Art and Architecture Students." *Art Documentation* 25, no. 1(2006): 38–42.

Brown, John Seely. "New Learning Environments for the 21st Century: Exploring the Edge." *Change* 38, no. 5 (2006): 18–24.

Daley, Elizabeth. "Expanding the Concept of Literacy." *Educause Review* 38, no. 2 (2003): 33–40.

Davidson, Cathy N., and David Theo Goldberg. *The Future of Learning Institutions in the Digital Age.* Cambridge, MA: MIT Press, 2009.

Dutton, Thomas A. "The Hidden Curriculum and the Design Studio: Toward a Critical Studio Pedagogy." In *Voices in Architectural Education: Cultural Politics and Pedagogy*, edited by Thomas Dutton, 165–193. New York: Bergin & Garvey, 1991.

Freeman, Geoffrey T. *Library as Place: Rethinking Roles, Rethinking Space.* Washington, DC: Council on Library and Information Resources, 2005.

Gerke, Jennifer, and Jack M. Maness. "The Physical and the Virtual: The Relationship between Library as Place and Electronic Collections." *College & Research Libraries* 71, no. 1 (2010): 20–31.

Gibson, Craig, ed. *Student Engagement and Information Literacy*. Chicago: Association of College and Research Libraries, 2006.

Hahn, Jim. "Mobile Learning for the Twenty-First Century Librarian." *Reference Services Review* 36, no. 3 (2008): 272–288.

Schillie, Jane E., Virginia Young, and Susan A. Ariew. "Outreach through the College Librarian Program at Virginia Tech." *The Reference Librarian* 71 (2000): 71–78.

Seamans, Nancy H., and Paul Metz. "Virginia Tech's Innovative College Librarian Program." *College & Research Libraries* 63, no. 4 (2002): 324–332.

Shapiro, Jeremy, and Shelley K. Hughes. "Information Literacy as a Liberal Art." *Educom Review* 31, no. 2 (1996). http://net.educause.edu/apps/er/review/reviewarticles/31231.html.

Shirky, Clay. *Here Comes Everybody: The Power of Organizing without Organizations*. New York: Penguin, 2008.

Snyder, Jaime, Robert Heckman, and Michael J. Scialdone. "Information Studios: Integrating Arts-Based Learning into the Education of Information Professionals." *Journal of the American Society for Information Science and Technology* 60, no. 9 (2009): 1923–1932.

Traxler, John. "Defining, Discussing, and Evaluating Mobile Learning: The Moving Finger Writes and Having Writ. . . ." *The International Review of Research in Open and Distance Learning* 8, no. 2 (2007): 1–13.

Wallach, Ruth. "The Academic Art Library in the Age of Interdisciplinary Discourse." In *The Handbook of Art and Design Librarianship*, edited by Amanda Gluibizzi and Paul Glassman, 265–276. London: Facet, 2010.

Ward, Dane. "Revisioning Information Literacy for Lifelong Meaning." *Journal of Academic Librarianship* 32, no. 4 (2006): 396–402.

Index

Page numbers followed by t indicate table

Academic libraries: Alternate Reality Games (ARGs) and, 13; engaging international students with, 71–80; technology, engagement, and outreach in, 28–29; Twitter, social media, and, 29. *See also* Library ease of use and satisfaction; Undergraduates engagement with academic library
ACRL Instruction Section's Multilingual Glossary, 79
A.I. Artificial Intelligence (movie), 12
Allison-Shelley Collection, 68
Alternate Reality Games (ARGs): assessment and outcome of, 18–20; background and goal behind, 11–12; creating, 13–18; future plans for, 21; as learning and engagement tools, 12–13; lessons learned in developing, 20–21; New York Public Library and, 6
Apple iPads, 126–28
AR. *See* Augmented reality (AR)
ARG. *See* Alternate Reality Games (ARGs)
Art and architecture library, at Virginia Tech, 119–21, 124, 125, 126
Art libraries, in digital age, 123–25
Artworks, 10
Association of College and Research Libraries (ACRL) Information Literacy Competency Standards, 91
Augmented reality (AR), 11, 29–30

Bednar, Marie, 63
Bednar internship, 63, 67, 68, 69
Bennett, Charlie, 23
Broadcasting, of *Lost in the Stacks* radio show, 26
Brown, John Seeley, 121–22, 123
Browsing, act of, 124
Bucks. *See* Bucks County Community College (Bucks)
Bucks County Community College (Bucks), 105, 115
Bucks group, 107
Bucks Mashup Contest, 115
Bucks Student Research Conference, 114
Busacca, Ali, 69

Campus Compact's 2010 Member Survey Executive Report, 85
Campus office for international students, 74, 76, 82
Carter, Karl, 107
Cataloging medieval materials, 64
CATEA. *See* Georgia Tech Center for Assistive Technology and Environmental Access (CATEA)
Chancellor's Task Force for Student Success, 41, 42

Children's Hunger Alliance and Project READ, 86–87
Civic engagement, 85
The College Blue Book, 73
College of Architecture and Urban Studies (CAUS), 126
Common intellectual and community building, 41–49
Community engagement, 88–90
Community on campus, common read programs and, 42
CRAAP Test (Chico's Meriam Library), 87
Cronbach's Alpha index, 35, 35t, 36t
Cross-cultural awareness, raising, 79–80

The Daily Collegian, 15
Daley, Elizabeth, 124
Decherney, Peter, 106
Digital libraries, 31, 32. *See also* Academic libraries
Digital literacy, 7
Digital poster, 109
Digital poster assignments, 113
Digital resources, 123
Digital technologies, 124
Digitizing medieval materials, 64
DiMenna-Nyselius Library at Fairfield University, 75
Dini, Erin, 69
DIRTT walls, 8
Diversity/Global learning. *See* International students
Dlugosz, Jennifer, 69
Duke University: interviewing honors researchers at, 51–55; rewarding students' information-seeking behaviors, 55–59
Durden, Robert F., 56
Durden prize applicants, research essay questions, 61

Ease of use, Cronbach's Alpha Index and, 36t
Ease of Use Composite Score, 35t
EDT 110: Community Research Connections, 86–87, 88, 89, 90, 91, 92
Educational Gaming Commons, 13, 20
EDUCAUSE, 13
EDUCAUSE Annual Conference 2008, 106
eLearning virtual Bucks County Community College campus, 105
Electronic resources, users and, 33
e-library system, 32

Engagement: of college students with library, 85–91; community, 88–90; information literacy competency, 91–93; of international students with academic library, 71–80; library, 90–91; of users in academic libraries, 28–29
Engagement events, 4
English program for nondegree students, international students and, 76
ESL instructors, librarians and, 76, 80

Facebook, *Lost in the Stacks* radio show on, 25
FCC. *See* Federal Communications Commission (FCC)
Federal Communications Commission (FCC), 26
Ferguson, Michael, 42
First impression, creating, 3–5
Flap book, 67, 68
Focus groups, 95
Fröbel, Friedrich, 68
Fun, creating element of, 5–6

Games and gaming, introducing, 5–6
Gardner's theory of multiple intelligences, 106
Gehry Partners, LLP, 8
Georgia Tech: *Lost in the Stacks* and, 26; Office of Undergraduate Studies at, 27–28; research community of, 27; Twitter feed and, 29
Georgia Tech Center for Assistive Technology and Environmental Access (CATEA), 26–27
Goddard, Cody, 65–67
Gross, Samantha, 113
GVU Research Showcase, 27

Halo (video game), 12
Hamer, Donald, 63
Henisch Photo-History Collection, 65–66
Higher education enrollment, international students and, 71–73, 72t, 73t
Hobbs, Renee, 106

IDS. *See* Interdisciplinary Design Studio (IDS)
Illinois Institute of Technology, Paul V. Galvin Library at, 78
"I Love Bees," 12
Independent studies programs, undergraduates and, 63–70
Information Commons, 7
Information literacy, 85, 123

Information literacy awards, 55
Information literacy competency engagement, 91–93
Information literacy continuum, 2–3, 10
Information literacy skills, 14, 21, 56, 59
Information literacy standards, 7
Information-seeking behaviors, students' rewarding on, 55–59
Institutional Review Board, 3
Integration of Knowledge (INTG) Metapatterns course, 112
Interdisciplinary Design Studio (IDS), 67
International student clubs, Penn State University library and, 76
International students: engagement with academic library, 71–80; enrollment in higher education, 71–72, 72t, 73, 75; as face of the library, 77–78; library orientations and liaisons, 74–75; library partnerships with other campus units, 76; library programs and services for, 79–80; multilingual library services for, 78–79; national survey of academic libraries and, 72–75, 72t, 73t
International-themed book displays, for international students, 73, 73t
Internship programs, undergraduates and, 63–70
Interviews, of honors researchers at Duke University, 51–55, 60–61

Kansas State University, 30
Kenyon, Matt, 67
Knowledge Commons, 7, 8
Krochalis, Jeanne, 63

Lauricella, Cheryl, 86
Layar iPhone app, library users and, 30
LCD screen, mobile: for aquarium project, 27; use for user opinions, 29
Learning and engagement tools, Alternate Reality Games (ARGs) as, 12–13
Learning theories, 106, 107
"Learning to be" forms of engagement, 122, 125
LEC. *See* Library East Commons (LEC)
Lewis Science Library, Princeton University, 8
Liaison librarian, for international students, 74, 75
LibQUAL+, 27, 96
Librarian program (eBrarian), 112

Librarians: Alternate Reality Games (ARGs) and, 12; developing partnerships and, 76; at Duke University, 51–59; engaging students with academic libraries, 1; international students and, 75, 77–78; at Penn State University, 13
Library ease of use and satisfaction: introduction to, 30–31; literature review, 31–34; study on, 34–36, 35t, 36t; study results, 36–37, 37t; summary and conclusions, 37–38
Library East Commons (LEC), 28
Library engagement, 90–91
Library projects, international students and, 80
Library public service, international students and, 77, 78
Library resources, use of, 7, 52–59
Library services: to international students, 73t, 74, 75, 79, 80; marketing, 95
Library spaces: art and architecture library, Virginia Tech, 119–21, 124, 125, 126; art libraries in the digital age, 123–25; library as studio, 119, 121–23; mobilizing student engagement, 125–28; visual aspects of, 7–10
Licenses, radio stations and, 26
Listening Is an Act of Love (StoryCorp Foundation), 42
Listening Project, 41
Locke, Nancy, 65
Lost in the Stacks radio show, 23–24; beginning of, 23–24; broadcasting, streaming, and podcasting, 26; marketing, 25–26; process of, 24–25
Lower Bucks County Community College campus, 105, 116

Marketing, customer service role in, 4; *Lost in the Stacks* radio show, 25–26
Marketing Communications and Outreach Plan 2007/2008 (Pennsylvania State University Libraries, 2007), 99
Marketing plan development: about, 96; introduction to, 95–96; marketing steering team and student engagement, 96–99; MBA program partnership, 96–98; recommendations and summary, 101–2; undergraduate marketing interns and, 100–101
Marketing Steering Team group, 98–99
Maynard, Brian, 67, 68
McGonigal, Jane, 6

Media and Instructional Design Space (MInDSpace), 105; aiding faculty in assignment design, 108–9; collaborating with classes, 110–12; concluding note, 117; founding principles of, 106–8; impact on students, 112–15; introduction to, 105; mashup contest, 115–17
Media Commons, 7, 13, 14
Media literacy(ies), 7, 109, 110
MediaScape, 8
MInDSpace. *See* Media and Instructional Design Space (MInDSpace)
"Mobile learning," 128
Mobile technology, 126
Multilingual services, for international students, 73, 73t, 78–79
Multimedia resources, 106
Multiple intelligences, Gardner's theory of, 106

National Science Foundation (NSF), 27
National Service-Learning Clearinghouse, 85
National survey of academic libraries and international students, 72–74, 72t, 80–83
Negative correlation, 35
NEH grant, 67
Nesbitt, Sarah, 68–69
New media literacies, 105, 107
New media literacies institute, 108, 109
New media literacy assignments, 110–11, 113, 114
New media literacy instruction, 108, 110, 112, 113, 114
New media literacy projects, 105, 107, 108, 110
New media literacy skills, 111
New media projects, 107, 108, 111
New media resources, 106, 108, 109, 110, 111, 113
New York Public Library, 6
New York Times, 9
Nine Inch Nails (musical group), 12
Nittany Lion, 14, 15, 16
NSF. *See* National Science Foundation (NSF)

OCLC Environmental Scan: Pattern Recognition (OCLC Online Computer Library Center 2003), 96
OCOB initiative. *See* One Campus, One Book (OCOB) initiative
One Campus, One Book (OCOB) initiative, 41–42
Online Learning and Information Literacy Librarians, 112
Open House (Penn State University), 3–4, 5, 6, 13
Oral History Association Best Practices for Oral History guidelines, 43
Orientation, for international students, 73, 73t, 74–75
Outcomes: of Alternate Reality Games (ARGs), 18–20; service learning, 88
Outreach, in academic libraries, 28–29
Outreach librarians, for international students, 75

Partnerships development, librarians and, 76
Paterno, Joe, 17
Paul V. Galvin Library at the Illinois Institute of Technology, 78
Pearson's Correlation Coefficient statistical test, 35
Pease, Lesley, 9
Penn State Medieval Society, 64
Penn State's Schreyer Honors College, 67
Penn State's Undergraduate Exhibition, 55
Penn State's University Park campus party, 3
Penn State University Libraries, 55; developing marketing plan for, 95–102; librarians at, 13; Office of Global Programs and, 76; orientation for international students, 74–75; participation in LibQUAL+, 96; undergraduate internship programs, 63–70
Perception of Libraries and Information Resources: A Report to the OCLC Membership (OCLC Online Computer Library Center 2005), 96
Petersburg Listening Project, Alaska, 43
Physical spaces, art libraries and, 123–24
Podcasting, of *Lost in the Stacks* radio show, 26
Poll Everywhere, 29
Positive correlation, 35
Princeton University, Lewis Science Library at, 8
Principal Component Analysis, 36
Print publications, for international students, 73, 73t
Print resources, users and, 33
Prizes, events and, 5, 6
Probst, Max, 111
Proces, Paul, 110

Programming for international students, 73, 74, 76
Project READ, 86–87, 88, 89
Public libraries, using academic libraries *vs.*, 34
Puchalski, M., 115

Rabbit hole, 11–12, 14, 15
Radio programs. *See Lost in the Stacks* radio show
Rare Books and Manuscripts, Penn State University Library, internship programs at, 63
Real-time polling, engaging users with, 28–29
Reflection, as proof of engagement, 87–93
Regular services promotion, for international students, 73t
Reid-Walsh, Jacqueline, 67, 68
Remote access, resources and, 33
Research, libraries and, 31
Researchers at Duke University, interviewing, 51–55
Research library rock 'n' roll radio show. *See Lost in the Stacks* radio show
Research organization, researchers at Duke University and, 53
Research paper assignment, 109
Research prizes, 55
Research skills, Alternate Reality Games (ARGs) and, 13
Robert F. Durden Prize, 56, 57, 58, 59
Rosas, Carlos, 67
Rubin, Steven, 65

Schwab, Ted, 64–65
Service learning: defined, 85–86; EDT110: community research connections, 86–87; reflection as proof of engagement, 87–93
Services, to international students, 74
Simon, Andrew, 57
Simon, Susan, 106
Slivka, Jennifer, 69
Smeal College of Business's Marketing Department, 96
Social media, academic library and, 29
Special Collections Library at the Penn State University Library, 63–70
Spielberg, Steven, 12
Staff training, as program for international students, 73t, 74, 79–80
Stelts, Sandra, 66
Stelts-Filippelli Undergraduate Internship, 63

StoryCorp Project, 42
StoryCorps Foundation, 42
Storytelling, 42
Strategic planning, 95
Streaming, of *Lost in the Stacks* radio show, 26
Student disciplinary expertise. *See* Marketing plan development
Students: Alternate Reality Games (ARGs) and, 13, 14; engagement, service learning, and, 86; engagement in marketing plan, 95–102; Media and Instructional Design Space (MInDSpace) impact on, 112–15. *See also* International students
Students, talented, 63
Studio-based learning, 122
Subject specialist librarians, orientation and, 75, 79, 80
Syracuse University Library, 9
System effectiveness, 32

Teaching and Learning with Technology Roundtable (TLTR), 115
Technology, in academic libraries, 28–29
"The Beast," 12
"The Library and Film," 24
TLTR. *See* Teaching and Learning with Technology Roundtable (TLTR)
Toccafondi, David, 106
Tours, for international students, 74
"Transformations: Movement in Toys That Teach," 67
Transparency, 120
Traxler, John, 128
Twitter: Georgia Tech and, 29; *Lost in the Stacks* radio show on, 25

UAS Listening Project: collecting stories, 44–45; creating community, 45–48; launching the project, 44; library impact, 48; Listening Project development, 41–42; outcomes/future directions, 48–49; project planning/layout, 43
Undergraduate internship programs, at Special Collections Library at Penn State University Libraries, 63–70
Undergraduate research: engaging in, 51–59; virtual poster sessions for, 27–28
Undergraduates engagement with academic library: celebrating the visual, 6–7; first impressions, 3–5; information literacy continuum, 2–3; introducing games and

gaming, 5–6; visual aspects of library spaces, 7–10
Unfolding spatial registers, 120
The University Libraries Marketing Steering Team: Final Report 2007–2008, 3
University of Alaska Southeast (UAS). *See* UAS
University of California–Berkeley, 55
University of Georgia, 9
University of Massachusetts, Amherst Libraries, 75
University of Oregon, 55
University of Washington User Survey tool, 35
University of Wisconsin–Madison, 55
University of Wisconsin–Madison Undergraduate Symposium, 55
Upper Bucks County Community College campus, 105
User effectiveness, 32
User effort, 32
Users, augmented reality and, 29–30
User satisfaction: academic libraries and, 32–33; ease of access and, 34; factors influencing, 32; library service quality and, 33

Vedantham, Anu, 106
Video mashup assignments, 106, 109, 111, 113
Video mashup projects, 106
Virginia Tech, art and architecture library at, 8, 119–21, 124, 125, 126
"Virtual aquarium" project, 26–27
Virtual poster sessions, for undergraduate research, 27–28
Virtual reality, 11
Visual, celebrating the, 6–7
Visual Literacy Competency Standards, 7

Web-based Marketing Toolkit, 99
Website/webpage, as service for international students, 73t
Workshops, for international students, 73, 79
WREK, 23, 24, 25, 26
Wright State University, 86

"Year Zero," 12

About the Editor and Contributors

Loanne Snavely is head of Library Learning Services at Penn State University Libraries. She has a MLn (Master of Librarianship) degree from Emory University, an MST degree from the Rochester Institute of Technology, and a BS from Juniata College. Loanne coedited *Designs for Active Learning* and has published articles on information literacy, visual images and information literacy, and other aspects of teaching and learning in libraries in the *Journal of Academic Librarianship*, *RUSQ*, *portal*, and other journals as well as chapters in books. Loanne has been chair of the Association of College and Research Libraries (ACRL) Instruction Section and of the Executive Committee of the Institute for Information Literacy. In 2003, she received the Miriam Dudley Instruction Librarian Award.

Dawn Amsberry is a reference and instruction librarian at Penn State University Libraries–University Park. She has an MLS from San Jose State University and an MA in Teaching English to Speakers of Other Languages from Hunter College. She has been a children's and reference librarian in public and academic libraries and has taught English as a Second Language (ESL) and writing to adults. She has published journal articles and book chapters on multiple aspects of academic library services to international students.

Maureen Barry is the librarian for First-Year and Distance Learning Services at Wright State University in Dayton, Ohio. She received her MSLS from the University of North Carolina at Chapel Hill in 2005. She recently published an article in *C&RL News* and blogs at "Service Learning Librarian."

Emily Daly serves as the coordinator of Upper Level Instruction and is the librarian for the Program in Education at Duke University. She has also worked as a public library teen librarian and as high school media coordinator. Emily received an MSLS from the University of North Carolina at Chapel Hill. She published a chapter in ACRL's *Embedded Librarians: Moving Beyond One-Shot Instruction.*

Ameet Doshi, MLS, MPA, is the user experience librarian and assessment coordinator at the Georgia Institute of Technology in Atlanta, where he also serves as the subject specialist for the School of Economics. He has a master's degree in information science from the University of Tennessee, Knoxville, a second master's degree in public administration (MPA) with a concentration in higher education leadership from the University of North Carolina–Wilmington, and is a LEED Accredited Professional for Operations and Maintenance.

Jacqueline M. Fritz is Instructor, Learning Technologies Liaison at Bucks County Community College, Newtown, Pennsylvania, where she was previously the new media librarian. She holds her MS in library and information science from Drexel University. An internship at the University of Pennsylvania's Weigle Information Commons (WIC) in Philadelphia helped to shape her career path in library science and new media. At Bucks, where she teaches students and works with faculty to support instruction, her interest in using media resources and technology tools to facilitate learning in the library is in practice every day.

Wendy Girven received her MSLS from Clarion University of Pennsylvania. She is the public services librarian at the University of Alaska Southeast. Wendy has published in *Partnership: The Canadian Journal of Library and Information Practice and Research* and was named as an ALA Emerging Leader in 2010.

Lesley Moyo is the director for Research and Instructional Services in the University Libraries at Virginia Tech. She has also held faculty positions at the University of Zambia, the University of Zimbabwe, and the University of Botswana. Lesley has published and presented widely on libraries and technology, including highly cited articles in the *Electronic Library, Library Collections & Technical Services*, and *Information Technology for Development.* Lesley was recognized and honored as one of *Library Journal's* "Movers and Shakers 2003: The People Who Are Shaping the Future of Libraries."

Emily Rimland is an information literacy librarian at The Pennsylvania State University–University Park, where she enjoys providing instruction, reference, and outreach services to undergraduate students. She holds an MLIS from the University of Pittsburgh, and her research interests include the application of emerging technologies to library services, information literacy, and instructional technologies. She has written book chapters and journal articles on using emerging technologies and social networking for reference, outreach, and in teaching credit classes.

Sandra Stelts is the curator of Rare Books and Manuscripts in the Special Collections Library at the Pennsylvania State University Libraries. She holds a BA from Hiram College, has done graduate work in Penn State's Department of Art History, and was a curatorial assistant at the Palmer Museum of Art. She has published articles in the fields of art history and the history of photography and is the coauthor of a chapter in the forthcoming book *Burke in the Archive*. In 2010, she was the recipient of the McKay Donkin Award for Outstanding Contributions to Penn State Faculty.

Patrick Tomlin is head of the Art + Architecture Library at Virginia Tech. He received his MLS from the University of North Carolina at Chapel Hill, an MA in art history from Florida State University, and is completing his doctoral dissertation in art history from Northwestern University. He has presented on copyright and Open Access in the arts.

Gary W. White is head of the Department of Reference, Collections & Research at The Pennsylvania State University. He holds an MLS from Kent State University, an MBA in marketing from the University of Akron, and is ABD in the higher education doctoral program at Penn State. Gary is active in the American Library Association, where he is serving as RUSA president (2011–2012) and has been chair of the Business Reference and Services Section (2003–2004). He was presented with the Gale Cengage Award for Excellence in Business Librarianship in 2008. Gary was editor of the *Journal of Business & Finance Librarianship* from 2005–2010 and has published widely in journals, including *College & Research Libraries*, the *Journal of Academic Librarianship*, *Reference & User Services Quarterly*, and the *Journal of Marketing Management*.

WITHDRAWN